Bright Promise,
Failed Community

Bright Promise,
Failed Community

Catholics and the American Public Order

Joseph A. Varacalli

LEXINGTON BOOKS
Lanham • Boulder • New York • Oxford

LEXINGTON BOOKS

Published in the United States of America
by Lexington Books
4720 Boston Way, Lanham, Maryland 20706

12 Hid's Copse Road
Cumnor Hill, Oxford OX2 9JJ, England

Copyright © 2000 by Lexington Books
First paperback edition 2001

British Library Cataloguing in Publication Information Available

Library of Congress Cataloging-in-Publication Data

Varacalli, Joseph A.
    Bright promise, failed community : Catholics and the American public order /
Joseph A. Varacalli.
        p.   cm.
    Includes bibliographical references and index.
        1. Catholic Church—United States. 2. Christianity and culture—United States.
    3. Sociology, Christian (Catholic)—United States. I. Title.

BX1406.3 .V37 2001
282'.73'0904—dc21

                                                                    2001034434

    ISBN 0-7391-0086-6 (cloth : alk. paper)
    ISBN 0-7391-0292-3 (paper : alk. paper)

Printed in the United States of America

⊖™ The paper used in this publication meets the minimum requirements of American
National Standard for Information Sciences—Permanence of Paper for Printed Library
Materials, ANSI/NISO Z39.48–1992.

This book is dedicated to the four great women who have tried their best to keep me on the straight and narrow: to my deceased mother and mother-in-law, Theresa and Lillian, respectively; to my daughter, Theresa; and most importantly, to my ever loving wife, Lillian.

Contents

Foreword

Dr. Joseph A. Varacalli, who is probably America's premier Catholic sociologist, gives us here a short book that is a good basic assessment of the condition of American Catholicism as it concerns its effect on the public life of the United States. Perhaps even more importantly he provides a practical schema—which, while a realistic and in many ways an obvious course of action, he never contends will be easy to implement—to help recover some of the earlier possibility Catholicism had of shaping the American public order for the good.

Many theological writers, of course, have told us why mankind and individual nations need the One, True, Holy, Apostolic Church of Rome. Varacalli explains for us why, sociologically, this is so. He discusses the great, largely ignored (in the United States) corpus of the Church's social teachings, which provides for us the basis for true justice and a true community of friendship (what Pope John Paul II calls a "civilization of love"). This is something that has eluded us for much of our history, as first Calvinism and then different versions of liberalism have left us with a sociopolitical perspective that has lacked balance. He also shows us how the Church is needed for the following: to restore and enrich American culture (which would happen primarily through her leadership as the defender of the natural law, the embracing of which is essential to the restoration of our moral order); to help rejuvenate our free political order by stressing the principle of subsidiary and offering a set of mediating structures that give it life; and to shape the balanced, ethical, spiritual individuals that are needed to sustain a democratic republic or secure a good political life whatever its institutional character.

In his discussion of the needed role of the Church in any hoped-for restoration of American culture, Varacalli demonstrates a deep understanding of the nature and stakes in the much-talked-about culture war going on in the United States and the Western world. He recognizes that this war, at root, is a spiritual one, carried out in the natural order with the invisible involvement of powers and principalities. It is thus not a struggle that man can win alone, or without Christ's Church at the front of the columns. Indeed, Varacalli's awareness of this leads to his particularly admirable conclusion—which has animated the thinking of the Society of Catholic Social Scientists, which he co-founded and which was his brainchild—that it must be a Catholic foundation that America must be rebuilt on. By his analysis of the interconnection of sacred and secular in social affairs and the central role the Church must play, Varacalli proves himself to be in the tradition of Orestes A. Brownson, one of America's greatest political thinkers.

Even as Varacalli emphasizes the essentiality of the Church's role in rebuilding American life, he recognizes that the major impediment to it is within the American Church itself. He insightfully discusses why it has been ailing. He explains how it has been racked by division and dissent since Vatican II, and how its bishops have weakly led. The reason for the latter is one of the most perplexing questions in the history of American Catholicism, which Varacalli provides an insightful—although, he admits, preliminary—analysis of in chapter 10. He develops the familiar theme, although with the unique perspective of a sociologist, that a dangerous amount of leadership and influence in the American Church in the post-conciliar era has been exercised by its bureaucracies, which have promoted positions and practices that have damaged faith and morals.

I believe that Varacalli is entirely correct that there has never been a "Catholic moment" in American history, not even in the "heyday" of American Catholicism from 1945 to 1960. The latter at best can be said to have afforded the conditions that could have made possible the development of something approaching such a moment. A large part of what made that heyday possible was the now mostly decimated Catholic "plausibility structure" I will discuss below. During this heyday Catholicism had become perhaps the major institutional, philosophical, and attitudinal force holding back liberalism from engulfing all of American culture, which had by then infected so much of our religion and life. The essence of liberalism, as Pope Leo XIII astutely observed, is the notion of the *autonomous self*. It was in the resistance to this that Catholicism at that time seemed to have its best possibility of emerging as the predominant shaper of a sound culture and way of life in the United States. (This fact was recognized by no less than the eminent Father John Courtney Murray, S.J., whatever the other shortcomings of his thought.)

The crisis of the post-conciliar American Catholic Church is one precipitated, then, by the entry into it of the flood tides of liberalism. Varacalli characterizes this as a succumbing to a kind of Americanism—since liberalism had become the predominant ethos of American life—and correctly understands that, while different writers might quibble with the degree to which this is so, the destructive individualism at the core of liberalism has been a tendency in America since our beginnings.

It is Varacalli's awareness of this destructive character of liberalism that leads him to the conclusion that—in sharp disagreement with the sentiments that have so dominated American Catholicism since the Council (and so damaged it)—there is no compromising with this doctrine. There may have to be tactical accommodations, true, but ultimately liberalism cannot be the foundation for a good, enduring political community. The Catholic objective, as indicated above, should be nothing less than "re-establishing all things in Christ" (Eph.1:10)—including the political order.

As mentioned above, Varacalli stresses the great value of the Catholic plausibility structure, which was so painstakingly built up in the United States in the first two-thirds of this century. This has been a frequent theme in his writings, and is one of the most insightful points of his sociological inquiry. A plausibility structure might, loosely, be defined as an institutional framework that puts into practice Catholic belief and provides a set of institutional and other tangible reference points for Catholics to look to in order to keep carrying out their faith in their daily lives and, indeed, to help shape the character of their various endeavors. Many writers—especially converts of the pre-conciliar period—have written about the influence of the vibrant set of Catholic institutions then extant (parishes, hospitals, orphanages, schools, colleges, etc.) on the Catholic community and the larger society. Varacalli, in my judgment, rightly insists on the need for a restoration of this Catholic plausibility structure to make possible the rebuilding of Catholic life in America. In this book and in his other writings he successfully, from a social science standpoint, defends the need for such a structure—showing how it is crucial for the maintenance of common principles and the building up of any community of people—against the trenchant criticism of so many "progressive" Catholics that it would represent merely a return to a despised "ghetto Catholicism."

A Catholic plausibility structure provides the basis of Varacalli's larger practical schema of utilizing mediating structures to reevangelize our own Catholic people and to take the battle for Christian truth to the culture generally. In doing this, however, he rightly cautions about the dangers of accommodation, which I believe have diluted the Catholic message so many times in the past and, in fact, have at times outrightly surrendered it on the altar of American cultural imperatives. In this light, he speaks realistically about the possibilities and limitations of social action cooperation with evangelical Protestants.

Before coming to the conclusion that a structural approach to evangelizing the culture, emphasizing mediating structures, is the best immediate step, Varacalli gives careful and intelligent analysis to the entire question of what sociologically are the best alternative approaches. In this context, he considers also the role that the individual (i.e., one-on-one) and cultural (i.e., solid Catholics "reinfiltrating" key decision making domains of American society) approaches might play. While each has its place, he believes that a particular stress on the structural is preferable. This makes sense, considering that the concern in this book is the Catholic encounter with the American *public order*, and that even at the best of times Catholics did not have extraordinary success in infiltrating the higher echelons of the leading sectors of American life. Varacalli also provides a perceptive sociological judgment about the targeting of macro-evangelization efforts by the American Church in the immediate future: the focus should be on the increasingly unchurched, but basically sympathetic and open, working class.

Varacalli also shows himself a perceptive analyst of the subtleties of politics and political perspectives with his brief discussion of the significance, from the standpoint of a possible Catholic-spearheaded renewal of our public order, of the presidential candidacy of Patrick J. Buchanan and the latter-day populism it represents. Varacalli seems to have seen, sooner than I did, that the Buchanan effort was inspired by—at least in an indirect and insufficiently developed way—Catholic social teaching and held substantial promise for furthering its influence in our politics.

There are many other good things in this short volume. Dr. Joseph Varacalli's analysis and recommendations need to be read and pondered, more so because they represent a social scientist's effort, using major theoretical frameworks and approaches from this area of modern knowledge, to inform the most crucial large-scale question for current American Catholicism: how to evangelize both within the ranks of our co-religionists and without. Nothing less than the very future of American culture, of the American Church, and of the free character of our political order are the stakes. In my judgment, Varacalli's effort is among the best examples of what the intellectual apostolate, especially in the social sciences, can put forth in the service of the Church in these troubled times.

Stephen M. Krason
Department of Political Science
Franciscan University of Steubenville
Steubenville, Ohio

Preface

My initial interest in the general area of Catholics and public life developed as I wrote my doctoral dissertation on the sociological significance of the Catholic "Call to Action" Conference under such renowned scholars as Peter L. Berger, Edward A. Shils, and Henry J. Browne. This interest was later fueled by my summer 1987 participation in a National Endowment of the Humanities seminar, "Religion and Western Political and Ethical Thought," held at Princeton University under the direction of Paul E. Sigmund. However, it was Robert George, the distinguished professor of politics at Princeton University and founding first vice-president of the Society of Catholic Social Scientists, who first suggested to me that I extend further my interests in the area of American Catholics and public life by writing this full-length monograph. Written as a Nassau Community College—S.U.N.Y. sabbatical project during the spring of 1996, in its earliest formulation, *Bright Promise, Failed Community: Catholics and the American Public Order* was first read at the Fourth Annual Conference of the Society of Catholic Social Scientists, Franciscan University, Steubenville, Ohio, October 26, 1996. Dr. Gary Glenn, professor of political science at Northern Illinois University, and Dr. Jack Schrems, professor of political science at Villanova University, ably served as fellow panelists and discussants. A second, updated version, was delivered at a conference held at Nassau Community College—S.U.N.Y. on September 11, 1998, and co-sponsored by the Nassau Community College Sociology Club and the New York Metropolitan Chapter of the Society of Catholic Social Scientists. The following individuals served as discussants at this second conference: Rev. Robert Batule of the Theology Department at St. John's University, Donald J. D'Elia of the History Department of S.U.N.Y.—New Paltz, Donald Doyle of the Political Science Department of Molloy College, Monsignor George P. Graham of the Society of

Catholic Social Scientists, Anthony L. Haynor of the Sociology Department of Seton Hall University, Rick Hinshaw of the New York State Catholic Conference, Salvatore J. LaGumina of the History Department of Nassau Community College—S.U.N.Y., Monsignor George A. Kelly of the Fellowship of Catholic Scholars, George A. Morton of the *Parish Visitor*, Richard Renoff of the Sociology Department of Nassau Community College—S.U.N.Y., Frank Russo of the American Family Association, William Schroeder of the Nassau Community College Board of Trustees, and William Toth of the Seminary at Seton Hall University. Others who reviewed various drafts of the manuscript include: Robert N. Bellah of the Sociology Department of the University of California at Berkeley, Christopher Blum of the History Department of Christendom College, Monsignor Daniel S. Hamilton of the Fellowship of Catholic Scholars, Peter Feuerherd of the *Long Island Catholic*, James K. Fitzpatrick of *The Wanderer*, John Janaro of the Theology Department of Christendom College, E. Michael Jones of *Culture Wars*, Stephen M. Krason of the Political Science Department of Franciscan University at Steubenville, James Likoudis of Catholics United for the Faith, Mark Lowery of the Theology Department of the University of Dallas, Rev. Daniel O'Connell, S.J., of the Psychology Department of Loyola University of Chicago, Frank Morriss of *The Wanderer*, Diane Traflet of the Seminary at Seton Hall University, Kenneth D. Whitehead of the Fellowship of Catholic Scholars, and Joseph P. Wall of the Society of Catholic Social Scientists. I accepted much, but not all, of the critical feedback offered to me by the aforementioned scholars. This volume is clearly better for their suggestions; I remain, of course, solely responsible for any of its deficiencies.

This volume should be seen as an extension of a previous work, *The Catholic and Politics in Post-World War II America: A Sociological Analysis* (1995), a project commissioned by the Society of Catholic Social Scientists. It is an extension in the sense that the analysis moves away from the specific issue of Catholic political impotence to the broader question of why Catholicism has not significantly shaped civil society and the public sector in the United States.

I also would like to both thank and acknowledge Ignatius Press, Christendom Press, and Monsignor George A. Kelly for permission to quote from works of which they control the copyright. Quotes were reprinted from *The Battle for the American Church Revisited*, by Monsignor George A. Kelly, on pages 11, 21, 22, 23, and 39, copyright 1995 Ignatius Press, San Francisco. Quotes were also reprinted from *The Crisis of Dissent* by Gerard Morrissey, on pages 11, 12, 16, and 113, copyright 1985 Christendom Press, Front Royal, Virginia. Quotes were reprinted from *The Battle for the American Church* by Monsignor George A. Kelly on pages 15, 16, and 456, originally published by Doubleday Books, New York, in 1979, copyright Monsignor George A. Kelly.

Thanks should also be given to Anthony DeLouise of the Nassau Community College—S.U.N.Y. Department of Academic Computer Services and to Serena J. Leigh of Lexington Books for the assistance they afforded in the technical production of the manuscript. Additionally, I am appreciative of the editorial assistance afforded by Ginger Strader of Lexington Books. Finally, I owe my greatest debt to my wife, Lillian, for all she has done for me over the years, including typing all the various drafts of this monograph.

Introduction

"What Hath Social Science to Do with Catholicism?": Tertullian Revisited

The major thesis of *Bright Promise, Failed Community: Catholics and the American Public Order* is that, to date, Catholic America has essentially failed, in any significant way, to shape the American Republic. The "bright promise" of Catholic America lies in the vast, ever developing, ever more sophisticated tradition of social Catholicism and natural law thinking that could, in principle, serve both as a leaven in American society and as an alternative to the currently reigning and mostly sterile philosophies and ideologies that monopolize both the thought and policies that emanate from the American public square. Unfortunately, American society has never experienced a "Catholic moment"— the closest represented by the immediate post-World War II era—nor is it presently close to approximating one. The major reason for the current situation lies in the "failed community" of Catholic America, that is, an ineffective and dissent-ridden set of organizational arrangements that has not succeeded in adequately carrying and institutionalizing the Church's social doctrine both among the Catholic American populace and into the key idea-generating sectors of American life. Put another way, the required restoration of the American Republic presupposes a "successful," that is, orthodox, integrated, and sophisticated, community to serve as the carrier of Catholic social doctrine. My thesis is developed in the Introduction, fourteen chapters (some with subsections) and a concluding Note, all informed by perspectives derived from, or consistent with, a Catholic social science.

1

Catholic Social Doctrine in America:
Irony and Tragedy

Among many other subthemes, this volume chronicles what to the cynic is a delicious irony and what to the concerned and serious Catholic is a wasted opportunity of tragic proportions. On the one hand and since its inception during the Apostolic era, the Catholic faith has always evinced, as intrinsic to its very nature, a fundamental concern for the disenfranchised, for the building up of a vital community life, and for the construction of a well-ordered polity and society. As James Hitchcock, for instance, states:

> Traditional Catholicism was never indifferent to the social dimensions of religion, as manifested for example in the countless hospitals, orphanages, homes for the aged and other institutions operated by the Church....Nor has the Catholic tradition of social action been merely one of response to individual needs....Despite this long history, the social dimension of the Gospel was treated after the Second Vatican Council [by progressives]...as though it were an entirely new discovery, as though Catholics of earlier generations had been callously indifferent to suffering.[1]

In this sense, then, the much-quoted declaration in the important 1971 statement of the Synod of Bishops, *Justice in the World*, to the effect that "a concern for social justice...is a constitutive feature of the preaching of the Gospel" is little more than a restatement of eternal Church teaching in a lexicon that resonants with the modern day mind. Likewise, one can agree with the oft-cited claim that the 1891 publication of *Rerum Novarum* marked the Church's entrance into questions concerning the social order *only* if one understands that the type of formal and articulated analysis provided in the encyclical is proportionate to, and consistent with, the degree of modernization and "rationalization," following Max Weber's analysis,[2] found in the broader European society of the last turn of the century.

Having stated this, it is nonetheless true that the Catholic Church *has* given increased attention to the "social question" over the past one hundred years. This is neither surprising nor inconsistent given the Church's historical record of responding faithfully and intelligently to the spiritual and material needs of a changing social order. In the case of the development of the social doctrine of the Church, this response can be seen as the Church's logical and organic application of constant Christian principles to newly emerging historical and social-structural situations, that is, the creation of nation-states and, more recently, of an incipient international order.[3]

Nonetheless, there is an irony and wasted opportunity regarding Catholic social doctrine that has now come into play. On the other hand, never has the Catholic Church (and, by implication, the world) had, as it does today, such an impressive and rich deposit of articulated social doctrine from which to draw in the needed attempt to reconstruct a fast disintegrating and decomposing social order. Yet, at least relative to the immediate post-World War II era in America (and Europe), presently the Church (and world) is further away from being able to assimilate and creatively apply this vision. And this inability is directly tied to the internal dissent within those Catholic institutions and agencies that were once consciously created to implement this vision.

It is, of course, true that, *early* in its history, it would have been unrealistic to expect an immigrant Catholic Church in America to have been able to institutionalize strongly articulated and established traditions in either the social or intellectual apostolates. For one thing, early Church leadership reasonably felt that it had to deal first with the practical and daily needs of impoverished immigrants as well as with the basic organizational exigencies of establishing Catholicism in Protestant America. By the post-World War II era, however, one could state that American Catholicism *did* have a viable tradition of social Catholicism that was able, to a significant degree, to be successfully passed on, at least to the Catholic faithful, through its impressive, internally consistent, integrated and religiously orthodox set of Church-related institutions. "Those were the days" when Catholic college professors would integrate *Rerum Novarum* (1891) and *Quadragesimo Anno* (1931) into their lectures and when such approaches as "Catholic" philosophy, sociology, psychology, art, music, and literature were not considered obsolete and anachronistic.[4]

The irony/tragedy is that when American Catholicism had an effective mode of mediation, its social message was, relative to the present situation, weak. Now that the message is ever so stronger, more sophisticated, and much deeper, its necessary communications vehicle is almost totally emaciated with the result that today both the American Catholic population and the American public square are almost totally innocent of the Catholic social doctrine they so desperately require for both individual salvation and social survival.

Volume Summary

Utilizing a threefold distinction between *culture, institutional life,* and the *individual,* the focus of chapter 1 is on the determination of just how "successful" Catholic America and its citizens have been in shaping the American Republic. From the viewpoint of a vital, orthodox Catholicism, the diagnosis offered is quite unfavorable. Despite impressive indications that an increasingly larger percentage of citizens has little confidence in the performance of America's public sphere institutions and in the character of the latter's leaders—a distrust and cynicism that is largely justified and that can be explained by structural and cultural-moral developments—the second chapter argues that the American Catholic population is not in a position to provide American society much needed religiously based reforms given its own widespread internal secularization. This is followed by a chapter presenting the case that, with the establishment of corporate capitalism, the subjectivisms associated with the processes of modernity, and the decomposition of the single most important "carrier" of the natural law—that is, the Catholic Church—individualism as the key American value has seen itself progressively freed from *any* public orientation, focusing instead either on the narrow demands of one's occupation or the search for a privatized meaning and the pursuit of self-centered happiness. The result of all of this is an American society without an effective and moral guiding public theology/philosophy and one devoid, temporarily at least, of the possibility of replacing Protestant and secular understandings of individualism with Catholic principles such as "personalism" and "solidarity."

Chapter 4 makes the case that, given the inability of the leaders of the Catholic Church in America to keep its house together by effectively transmitting and evangelizing the Catholic worldview, external ideologies (e.g. feminist, socialist, capitalist, therapeutic, new age, homosexual, etc.) have made strong internal inroads into the Church, both structurally and attitudinally, thus polarizing and factionalizing the Mystical Body of Christ. Put another way, the winning—to date—progressivist secular worldview in the present broader American culture war has been passively absorbed by the winning—to date—liberal Americanist side in the contemporary "battle for the American Church." The next chapter addresses the issue of how orthodox Roman Catholics should be expected to relate to contemporary conservative Protestantism *politically* (cooperatively), *culturally* (ambivalently), and *theologically* (critically). Theologically, only the Catholic Church can claim to be the fullest expression of the Church of Christ while, sociologically, Catholicism is the only vehicle that satisfactorily expresses and adequately relates to each other the various dimensions of true religion. That the natural law exists and has perennially existed is an important theme in chapter 6, which also argues that prevalent modernist modes of thought have denied this reality with the consequence of making it much more difficult for the average individual to direct himself toward both acknowledging and conforming to the objective moral order. Put another way, Catholicism in post-Vatican II America lacks the required internal integrity and consistency to adequately represent the natural law in the American polity and civil society.

Chapter 7 argues that while the Catholic vision is a wondrously complex thing to contemplate in all of its majesty and subtlety, it is a vision even harder to institutionalize in the rounds of everyday existence. This vision requires a certain set of supportive institutional arrangements—called by sociologists a "plausibility structure"—to keep all of its complex elements in their proper balance and relationship and with a necessarily vital "accent on reality." Given the present battering of the Church's plausibility structure in the United States, due to both external and internal forces, what sociologically shapes the majority of Catholic citizens is not the "mind of the Church" but the prevalent cultural messages of an ever more secular, materialistic America. The next chapter sympathetically investigates but rejects the thesis that post-World War II American Catholicism represented an authentic "Catholic moment." A 1950s Catholicism can best be seen as anticipating an authentic Catholic moment, a moment further away at this writing then it was at that time due, primarily, to unnecessary self-inflicted wounds to the Catholic body and despite the grand vision of Vatican II and the writings and stature of John Paul II. An authentic "Catholic moment" in America requires a far more radical remodeling of the society along Catholic lines than has hitherto historically been the case.

The analysis offered in chapter 9 provides evidence that what has occurred within Catholicism during the post-Vatican II era is an example of a pervasive "secularization from within," that is, when traditional religion survives in society as a hollowed out, ineffective reality, little more than providing a thin veneer for what is actually and effectively nonreligious belief and activity. Offered are examples of this operating in terms of (a) general theological worldview, (b) within the national headquarters of the National Conference of Catholic Bishops/United States Catholic Conference, and (c) within the other major institutions of Catholic life. In the next chapter, the case is made that, as a body, the American Catholic bishops have failed in exercising their duties. Certain *demographic, historical, social-structural, ideational, cultural,* and *characterological* factors that partially explain this failure are explored. Given the increasingly hostile nature of American public sphere institutions (e.g., the three branches of government, corporate capitalism, education, the mass media, and the arts) toward an authentic Catholicism, the issue of the proper manner of Catholic participation in our society is addressed in chapter 11. While rejecting the underlying vision of America as embraced by neoconservatives, the argument is presented that Catholic restorationists should utilize the neo-conservative "mediating structures" approach as the main method "to restore American civilization to Christ." In the application of this "mediating structures" approach, "Church-like," "sect-like" and "individualistic" responses, it is argued, can be utilized provided that these postures are thoroughly informed by the Catholic faith, properly understood, and consciously complement and supplement each other.

Chapter 12 addresses the issue of which sectors of American society, sociologically speaking, are ripe for conversion to the faith and which are not. Prominent in the discussion is the claim that an unexplored and propitious area of evangelization lies within the millions of basically unchurched and nominal Christians who are part of America's working classes. The next chapter provides an account of the partially successful, partially failed attempt to restore the Catholic Church in the United States since the pontificate of John Paul II. The final chapter provides an analysis of how Catholicism, theoretically and actually, contributes to American society (a) through the promulgation of the social doctrine of the Church and the supporting of the natural law, (b) by offering a series of "mediating structures" that operate between the individual and the

State/megastructures of public life, and (c) by shaping individuals characterized by holiness, intellectualism, aesthetic appreciation, and a social consciousness. The concluding Note reaffirms that the basic duty of faithful Catholics is to stay the course for Christ, His Church, and His human creation, at whatever cost and regardless of which direction the current worldly winds blow.

Catholicism and Social Science

Many in the early Christian community, influenced greatly by the eschatological hopes for an imminent return of the Lord, basically posited a fundamental disjunction between Christianity and the world, rejecting everything of a this-worldly nature. In H. R. Niebuhr's famous classificatory scheme, such a posture represents the "Christ against culture" option, an option still accepted today by certain Protestant sects in the Anabaptist tradition.[5] Theologically, this position was represented by Tertullian who rhetorically asked: "What has Athens [i.e., the world]…to do with Jerusalem [that is, God]?"

The Catholic Church, at least since the third century A.D., has rejected the "Christ against culture" option accepting in its place a model whose goal is "to restore all things in Christ." This Catholic model serves as the true *via media* between all the other empirically available options regarding the relationship between God and society. It is one that rejects either a too facile acceptance or denial of the world and its social institutions. It is one that rejects either overplaying or underplaying the respective role of faith or of reason in religious and human affairs. It is one that rejects either conception of man as completely good or as all being equally depraved. It is one that sees the locus of salvation as otherworldly but requiring a great deal of this-worldly effort in the name of Christ.

Translated into a focal concern of this monograph, the Catholic task is, *first*, to transform secular social science and, *then*, to utilize it in order to further the universal missions of the Church, geared to the salvation of all souls and to the betterment of all humanity. The Catholic appropriation of the social sciences sets itself in sharp relief from either of its two major alternatives, what I've termed the *ideological* and *positivistic* models.[6]

While a significant percentage of American social scientists claim that their primary task is to produce, *qua scholar*, "objective" research about the social world, this percentage has undoubtedly declined since the 1960s, an era that initiated the institutionalization of overtly ideologized forms of sociology (e.g., Marxism, feminism), which claim that social research is a mere means to promote some specifically this-worldly end (e.g., socialism, the "androgynous" society).[7] The latter perspective assumes not only that the political cause in question is of more importance than the integrity of the scholarly process but also that the reality that the philosophy and personal values of the researcher affects the nature of the research process makes the goal of objectivity an impossible one. In the final analysis, this camp argues, if all intellectual activity is ideology and the political cause is supreme, then "objectivity" as a goal must be viewed only as a clever rationalization and intellectual tool used by the guardians of the status quo to stamp out the virtuous utopian impulse. It is the case, of course, that Catholicism, with its belief in an objective moral order and the power of reason to grasp truth, rejects this ideological, that is, subjectivist, politicized, historicist, "post-modern," model.

Unfortunately, Catholic social thought does not find a comfortable home in the major alternative camp of positivism. Positivism, while arguing for objectivity, depicts the human being—and more to the point, the individual scholar—as devoid of free will, creativity, and responsibility. As such, the positivistic sociologist denies that the philosophy and personal values of the scholar impact on the research enterprise. Social science, in other words for the positivist, is "value-free." The Catholic sensibility, on the contrary, would argue that while the goal of social science is to produce objective social research, objectivity is attained, or at least closely approximated, through consciously understanding precisely how one's philosophical, theological, and value commitments impact on the intellectual pursuit of truth.

The Catholic scholar fits in well *neither* with the ideological or positivistic model of social science research. Accepted from the former is the claim that the "cause"—in the case of Catholicism, the salvation of souls—is ultimately more important than any scholarly effort. However, rejected from the ideological camp is the claim that objectivity in social research neither can nor should be sought after. It *can* be sought because *reason, albeit operating through culture*, has the ability to ultimately transcend any ideological moorings and reach a transcendent Truth. It *should* be sought—contra Tertullian—because the pursuit of truth, albeit a penultimate allegiance in the Catholic worldview, is a good in and by itself. Accepted from the positivist camp, on the contrary, is the claim that objectivity can and should be the goal of the sociologist qua scholar. Rejected from this model, however, is the denial that the scholar, with his/her worldview, is an active participant in the research enterprise.

Viewed from the perspective of this monograph, social science is not a completely autonomous discipline; the empirical facts about the social world that the social scientist is concerned with discovering and gathering are influenced by values. The scholar should approach, then, the quest for an objective understanding of social reality through the recognition and taking into account of how values impact on the various stages of the research process. There are at least five such impacts. They are: (1) the *motivation*, or, in many cases, the *ideological agenda* of the individual researcher, (2) what the researcher considers (or doesn't consider) to be either a worthy *research project* or *social problem* to be alleviated, (3) the *analytical concepts, definitions,* and *theoretical frameworks* that the researcher either creates or decides to employ, (4) how the researcher chooses to *interpret* data or, conversely, what aspects of social reality the researcher considers irrelevant in analysis, and (5) what the researcher considers to be possible *social policy* recommendations.[8]

This fivefold classificatory scheme of the impact of values on the social scientific enterprise is immediately relevant to the overall thesis (and multitude of subthemes) found in *Bright Promise, Failed Community: Catholics and the American Public Order*. Regarding the overall thesis, this volume clearly makes the case that one major reason that Catholics haven't restored American civilization to Christ is because they haven't sufficiently developed Catholic approaches to the social sciences and then applied them to American public policy. These are the two major goals of the newly established—in 1992— Society of Catholic Social Scientists.[9]

Only a few examples of such applicability to the subthemes can be offered at this point. Regarding the first issue of *motivation*, isn't it obvious that "Americanist" Catholic sociologists like Rev. Andrew M. Greeley desire to substitute an idolatrous embrace of the American nation for allegiance to the historic faith of the Catholic religion? Isn't it obvious that many secular sociologists are motivated by a desire to destroy the very same traditional nuclear family that is assumed in *Familiaris Consortio* to be the natural form of mankind? Isn't it also obvious that the leaders of corporate capitalistic America are motivated in their thinking and actions by a desire to maximize profits and are, in the main at least, either indifferent to the needs of workers for gainful and dignified employment or, at best, see it as a decidedly secondary concern? Conversely put, isn't it obvious that Catholic social scientists applying their skills to the pro-life movement are motivated by their respect for truth and an objective moral order and love for all of God's creation, including the most defenseless?

Regarding the second issue of what is defined as an important *research project*, isn't it obvious that many progressive Catholic scholars and elites do not see a crisis in the way doctrine and catechesis are taught in Catholic schools, parishes, and seminaries? Or that many do not accept the Church's teaching on homosexuality and birth control? Isn't it the case that many secular social scientists do not consider widespread abortion and euthanasia to be "social problems"? How many progressive Catholic or secular social scientists would consider it to be worthwhile to empirically study the salutary effects of Natural Family Planning on marriage? Or, for that matter, how many are truly open to uncovering the deleterious effects of many sex education courses?

Regarding the third set of issues that deal with *concepts, definitions*, and *theories*, it is clear that many progressive Catholic and secular scholars choose theoretical frameworks that emphasize the inevitability of conflict and exploitation in society and in social relations over those that stress order, interdependence, and complementarity. Such models, as but one example, oftentimes exaggerate or disproportionately focus on what goes wrong in marriages and traditional nuclear families. Progressive Catholic thinkers, relatedly, tend to view legitimate authority in the Church not as an expression of love and fidelity to Christ but as the crude and immoral exercise of naked power. Secular and progressive Catholic thinkers also tend to uncritically accept those theoretical frameworks (e.g., Marxism, Freudianism, feminism, deconstructionism) that reduce out of existence ány affirmation of the supernatural. Similarly, they tend to embrace models positing the human actor as *homo economicus*. How many secular and progressive Catholic social scientists, conversely, make reference to the idea of natural law and to such concepts as personalism, subsidiarity, and solidarity? Linguistic definitions, relatedly, are also very important to analyze. Progressive Catholics tend to wrap up social justice issues in socialistic lingo and tend to accept broad (and unfair) definitions of such terms as "homophobia," "racism," and "anti-Semitism."[10]

Regarding the fourth issue of interpretation, isn't it true that many progressive Catholic and secular social scientists choose to emphasize the alleged "liberating" consequences for women of full participation in the labor force while conveniently ignoring the empirical evidence regarding the negative emotional and physical consequences for children who are placed for long periods in day-care centers? Or that they would legitimize what is, in actuality, pathological "life-style alternatives in family living" while cavalierly dismissing the destruction ushered forth by an increasingly "fatherless America"?[11] Conversely put, it is much more likely that orthodox Catholic social scientists would lampoon the claims that divorce is an uncontested "natural right" and that the children of divorce do not suffer negative emotional and economic consequences.

Regarding public policy, fifthly and finally, Catholic social scientists would be far less apt to suggest social reforms for the American Republic that assume either the (capitalist) image of "autonomous man" or the (socialist) claim that the State is the ultimate authority in earthly affairs. Put another way, a society informed by Catholic social policy would allow neither "assisted suicide" as an individual "right," nor a government engineered eugenics program. Putting the issue of the impact of values on the research process in a more positive light, it can be stated that, in principle, social science itself can be Catholicized through the incorporation of valid and true values that are either Catholic or are consistent with the Faith. The calling of a "Catholic social science" is:

> (a) to provide objective social research (b) in assisting the Catholic Church in the tasks of (1) understanding how surrounding social forces affect the Faith and (2) reconstructing the social order along Christian principles (c) by applying, where appropriate, Catholic principles and a Catholic sensibility to the existing body of sound social scientific theory, concepts, and methods and (d) through a thorough public intellectual exchange.[12]

Regarding point "a," a Catholic social science rejects all forms of "ideological" or "politically correct" thought, that is,, thought concerned with supporting the material interests of any group by distorting a truthful depiction of social reality. Accepted is the claim that there is an objective social order, an understanding of which can be closely approximated through the critical application of reason.

Regarding point "b," a Catholic social science can assist legitimate ecclesiastical leadership in at least two ways. The first is in the understanding of how social and historical processes and events impact on developments within the Church. The second is by suggesting a range of acceptable social policies and programs geared to both Church and society that are universal in import and accord with Catholic social doctrine.

Regarding point "c," accepted is the claim that some substantial part of the secular social scientific tradition is valid and useful. Analogous to the argument that the light of the Gospel as mediated through the Church's Magisterium perfects the natural reasoning power of the pagan, a Catholic social science believes that the incorporation of distinctive Catholic principles (e.g., subsidiarity, personalism, solidarity) and the influence of a general Catholic worldview can serve as a leaven to social science as it presently exists.

Regarding point "d," rejected is the notion that all that is necessary for an immediately resurrected social science profession is the substitution of the "right" Catholic values for the "wrong" secular values. If a Catholic social science is to become a successful tool for both substantive understanding and evangelization, it must actively confront, through frank comparison and honest analysis, the countervailing values, theories, concepts, methodologies, and arguments of secular social science. The Church's stance vis-à-vis secular social science must be the stance she has historically taken toward the world: reject error, search for compatibilities, co-opt when useful, and create anew when necessary.

Hopefully, such a frank and public intellectual exchange between secular and Catholic social science will move in the direction of institutionalizing a universal theoretical framework for the social sciences based on the natural law[13] and one consistent with Holy Scripture and a Sacred, yet evolving, Church Tradition. At the very least, the establishment of Catholic perspectives in the social sciences would guarantee the Church a presence within both the intellectual marketplace and those arenas in which public policy is forged. The ultimate goal, however, is for a fully developed and articulated Catholic social science to serve as an important vehicle for the social reconstruction of American society derived from, or at least consistent with, the principles of Catholic social doctrine.

Notes

1.   James Hitchcock, *The Pope and the Jesuits* (New York: National Committee of Catholic Laymen, 1984), 125-126.

2.   Max Weber, *The Theory of Social and Economic Organization* (New York: Oxford University Press, 1947); *From Max Weber*, Hans Gerth and C. Wright Mills, eds. (New York: Oxford University Press, 1946).

3.   Joseph A. Varacalli, "Whose Justice and Justice for What Purpose? A Catholic Neo-Orthodox Critique," *International Journal of Politics, Culture, and Society* 6, no. 2 (winter 1992): 316. Stephen M. Krason, *Liberalism, Conservatism, and Catholicism: An Evaluation of Contemporary American Political Ideologies in Light of Catholic Social Teaching* (New Hope, Kentucky: Catholics United for the Faith, 1991).

4.   Joseph A. Varacalli, "'Those Were the Days': Church and Society in the 1940s and 1950s," *Faith and Reason* 16, no. 1 (spring 1990): 81-89.

5.   H. R. Niebuhr, *Christ and Culture* (New York: Harper and Row, 1951).

6.   Joseph A. Varacalli, "Secular Sociology's War against *Familiaris Consortio* and the Traditional Family: Whither Catholic Higher Education and Catholic Sociology?" in *The Church and Universal Catechism*, Rev. Anthony J. Mastroeni, ed. (Steubenville, Ohio: Franciscan University Press, 1992), 161-186.

7.   Anthony L. Haynor and Joseph A. Varacalli, "Sociology's Fall from Grace: The Six Deadly Sins of a Discipline at the Crossroads," *The Quarterly Journal of Ideology* 16, nos. 1-2 (June 1993): 3-29.

8.   Varacalli, "Whose Justice," 311.

9.   Joseph A. Varacalli, "The Society of Catholic Social Scientists: Catholic Social Science and the Reconstruction of the Social Order," *Faith and Reason* 22, nos. 1-2 (spring-summer 1996): 3-14. Stephen M. Krason and Joseph A. Varacalli, "The Society of Catholic Social Scientists: Calling and Invitation," *Social Justice Review* 84, nos. 1-2 (January-February 1993): 3-4.

10.   Joseph A. Varacalli, "Catholic Social Science, Language, and William Brennan: Initial Reflections and Key Questions," in *Language and Faith*, Rev. Anthony J. Mastroeni, ed. (Steubenville, Ohio: Franciscan University Press, 1997), 77-90.

11.   Joseph A. Varacalli, "Review Essay on David Blankenhorn's *Fatherless America: Confronting Our Most Urgent Social Problem*," *Faith and Reason*, forthcoming. Joseph A. Varacalli, "Review Essay on Judith Wallerstein and Sandra Blakeslee's *Second Chances: Men, Women, and Children A Decade After Divorce*," *Fellowship of Catholic Scholars Newsletter* 13, no. 1 (December 1989): 17-19.

12.   Joseph A. Varacalli, "Sociology, Catholicism, and Andrew Greeley," *Lay Witness* 13, no. 9 (June 1992): 1-6.

13.   John Finnis, *Natural Law and Natural Rights* (Oxford: Clarendon Press, 1980), 18.

Chapter One

Catholics and "Success" in the Contemporary American Republic: All That Glitters Is Not Gold

"Success," oftentimes viewed as an end unto itself, is more properly seen as a *means* to some end, whether that end is defined in spiritual or material terms. This fundamental point must be borne in mind when attempting to determine just how "successful" contemporary Catholic citizens are in the American Republic. Moreover, a threefold distinction between *culture, institutional life*, and the *individual* can be usefully applied in this determination.

Catholics and American Culture

First, how successful have Catholics been in shaping the larger American *culture*? Contemporary Catholic America has conformed much more than challenged the basically secular nature of the present American culture.

Example Number One: The Family

Taking an example of importance, it is now widely acknowledged that the present-day weakening of American family life has produced numerous social and personality pathologies (e.g., suicide, drug abuse, criminal activity, juvenile delinquency, welfare dependency, low-level educational achievement, poor character formation, and emotional and psychiatric problems of one sort or another). One would think that a Catholic subculture would serve as an important break to this general movement given that, as Gallup and Castelli state, "family life has always been at the heart of Catholicism."[1] However, Gallup and Castelli report that:

> The make-up of American Catholics is changing in terms of family status. The percentage of Catholics who are married has dropped since 1976, while the percentage that are single, separated, or divorced has increased...one Catholic teenager in four say that their natural parents have been divorced, the same rate found in the general population. . . . Catholics have historically favored larger families than have other Americans, but by 1985 the difference in ideal family size between Catholics and Protestants had disappeared as Catholics became part of the mainstream, which considered two children the ideal family size. . . . American Catholics have favored access to contraceptives and information about them in the same proportion as the rest of the population since the 1950s.[2]

At another juncture in their analysis, they state that "in 1969, 72 percent of American Catholics said they believed that pre-marital sex was morally wrong...but by 1985, only 33 percent said...so."[3] Family disintegration has occurred, then, despite a significant tradition of Catholic social thought (e.g., *Casti Connubii*, *Humanae Vitae*, and *Familiaris Consortio*) and natural law thinking which, in principle, could enrich and, indeed, save an American civilization now in the process of unraveling.

Example Number Two: Capitalism and Socialism

A second example of how Catholics in America have failed to shape American culture can be found in their changing historical relationship to the two currently reigning non-Catholic ideologies of the public sphere of life, that is, capitalism and socialism. In his encyclical, *Sollicitudo Rei Socialis* (1987, #21), Pope John Paul II reaffirms that

> the Church's social doctrine adopts a critical attitude towards both liberal capitalism and Marxist collectivism. For from the point of view of development the question naturally arises: in what way and to what extent are these two systems capable of changes and updatings such as to favor or promote a true and integral development of individuals and peoples in modern society? In fact, these changes and updatings are urgent and essential for the cause of a development common to all.[4]

Applying the encyclical to America, one can state that the American public square is divided basically into two powerful ideological blocs, that is, capitalism and socialism, both hardening into "structures of sin" incompatible, *as they presently exist*, with the Catholic faith. American capitalist elites—the old business class—tend to be driven by an "all consuming desire for profit" and have generated among the middle class a "civilization of consumerism."

American socialist elites—the new knowledge class—in turn, are primarily driven by an absolutist held "thirst for power" that has produced among the lower classes (especially but not exclusively) a debilitating dependency on both government and its gnostic-like leaders as well as numerous social pathologies such as fatherless families and violent crime. Both capitalist and socialist concepts of development, furthermore, are deficient because, among other things, they tend to identify development with economic factors, ignoring or downplaying its necessary social, cultural, moral, and transcendent religious dimensions. Rev. Andrew M. Greeley is correct when he asserts that "Catholic social theory must be profoundly skeptical of all attempts at 'modernization' or 'development' that purport to improve the material lot of people by destroying its culture and social structure."[5] (A useful and even-handed attempt to provide an analysis of the strengths and weaknesses of both capitalism and socialism can be found in Peter L. Berger's *Pyramids of Sacrifice*; his analysis awaits an orthodox Catholic critique.)[6]

Early in their history, Catholics in America, from the immigrant through its working class to lower middle-class periods, tended to be both suspicious about and pragmatic in their allegiance toward either capitalism or socialism. This was the result of either their naturally endowed "common sense" and natural law thinking (pagan style) or inculturation into Catholic social doctrine. As Catholics, however (and as a general rule) have become more middle to upper-middle class, they have, unfortunately, followed the social-psychological lines of least resistance, embracing either of the two secular alternatives. As such, a great evangelistic opportunity has been missed. A large, formally educated, middle-class Catholic Church, armed with millions of advocates and practitioners of Catholic social doctrine could have transformed American civilization by either structurally reforming both capitalism or socialism or perhaps even by providing some third alternative.

On the present scene, it is perhaps only Patrick J. Buchanan, through his advocacy of a "conservatism of the heart," that has attempted to provide some quasi-Catholic alternative to the deformed ideologies facing Americans.[7] While basically accepting the broad framework of what Michael Novak[8] would term a "democratic capitalist" society, Buchanan—a self-proclaimed "limited government populist"[9]—would nonetheless reform capitalism through selective government intervention designed to protect jobs, families, and communities and through the insistence that noneconomic values are, in the final analysis, more important than simple aggregate economic growth. While only one possible Catholic alternative, Buchanan's approach, it can be plausibly argued, incorporates such fundamental Catholic concepts as subsidiarity, solidarity, and the universal purpose of goods as applied internally to the American nation-state. The distinguished Catholic intellectual, Charles E. Rice, agrees. As he states:

On various issues, including particularly abortion and free trade, Buchanan offers a vision which takes proper account of the nature of the human person. He is not afraid to affirm the dignity of that person as created in the image and likeness of God and with an immortal destiny that transcends the interests of the state....Buchanan reminds us that the "bottom line" of the utilitarians is not really the bottom line at all. He reminds us that the common good of a nation...requires policies to foster the family and local communities. In contrast, the abstractions of global free trade operate today to enhance the arbitrary power of international bureaucracies for whom the human person is merely an interchangeable economic unit.[10]

On the issue of immigration, Buchanan clearly favors the interests of the American nation/worker over those of both the elite architects of the "new world order" and millions of needy would-be immigrants. This latter fact raises the issue of the compatibility of Buchanan's vision with the Catholic principle of the universal purpose of goods as applied to what the Church has written regarding the obligation of wealthier to poorer countries. The American Catholic Lawyers Association, for one, argues that Buchanan's position does not contradict Church teaching but is debatable within an authentic Catholic framework.[11] Further systematic and objective research and honest and open debate is necessary on this issue.[12]

Whither Catholic Social Theory and Practice?

Although disagreeing with the dates he offers (which make it appear that *serious* secularization among Catholics started prior to Vatican II), Rev. Andrew Greeley is essentially on the mark when he declares that

> sometime between 1955 and 1970, Catholic social theory vanished from the scene, and Catholics with social concerns were forced to choose between capitalism and socialism. Since the latter is by far the more fashionable of the two ideologies, Catholics have opted for soft-core socialism and have allied themselves with revolutionary forces. Of course, most of these would-be revolutionaries are college professors, bureaucrats, or clergy persons, and their revolutionary activity never goes beyond talk. They issue statements, write articles, and testify at U.S.C.C. (United States Catholic Conference) hearings, but they never *do* much of anything.[13]

The "bright promise" of Catholicism in America has not been fulfilled. The important ideas of Catholic social doctrine lay, for the most part, dormant, not being taught and lacking a sufficient mode of effective communication throughout both Catholic and non-Catholic America. As a matter of fact and compounding the depressing situation, the general Catholic population—including, of course, millions of nominal Catholics—is, relatively speaking, oblivious to the unraveling and decaying public order. As Gallup and Castelli report, "Catholics have consistently...been slightly more satisfied [than have Protestants]...with the state of the nation."[14] Such a finding, of course, is quite consistent for a subculture uncritically accepting of, and striving for, "success" as defined by whomever and whatever is shaping the larger society.

Catholics and Institutional Life

Second, how successful have Catholics been in creating, maintaining, and developing a mutually interdependent set of *institutions* (e.g., parish, seminary, educational, health care, mass media, professional and other assorted voluntary associations) that serve both to successfully socialize baptized Catholics into an authentic understanding of the faith and to represent effectively—in a cultural, social, and political sense—Catholicism within the decision-making arenas of the megastructures of American society (e.g., government, corporate America, the mass media, the arts, the educational establishment)? The institutions of Catholic America have suffered a massive "secularization from within" in the post-Vatican II period and have, as such, failed in their dual purposes. The "failed community" of contemporary Catholicism explains one blindspot and weakness of Rev. Richard Neuhaus's thesis about the "Catholic moment" in America.[15]

Writing in 1987 as a Lutheran theologian who liked to describe himself as an Evangelical Catholic, Pastor Richard J. Neuhaus argued that "this...is the moment in which the Roman Catholic Church in the world can and should be the lead church in proclaiming and exemplifying the Gospel. This can and should also be the moment in which the Roman Catholic Church in the United States assumes its rightful role in the culture-forming task of constructing a religiously informed public philosophy for the American experiment in ordered liberty."[16] Years later, after a conversion to the Catholic faith and then entering the priesthood, Rev. Neuhaus reflects on and elaborates further his now famous thesis:

> Seven years ago, I published a book, *The Catholic Moment*, in which I contended that the premier responsibility for the Christian mission rests with the Catholic Church—the premier opportunity, and therefore responsibility, for evangelization and cultural transformation in America and the world. I am regularly asked whether I think *the* Catholic Moment is now past. The answer is emphatically "No." I say this in part because, if the Catholic Church is what she claims to be, every moment, from Pentecost until our Lord returns in glory, is *the Catholic Moment*. I say this in part because my "reading of the signs of the times" suggests that the world is newly open to, newly hungry for, a sure word of truth and hope, a word that is most certainly possessed and most convincingly presented by the Catholic Church.[17]

While Rev. Neuhaus is correct in that the necessary Catholic ideas are available for the transformation of American society, he fails to address satisfactorily the need for the existence of a set of institutional carriers for those ideas. Presently these institutions have lost their cohesiveness, integrity, and effectiveness, given the uncritically assimilationist "Americanizer"[18] or "Americanist"[19] takeover of large sections of Catholic America. Conversely put, the institutionalization of any "Catholic moment" in American society presupposes an internal orthodox restoration within the Catholic community. No less a light than Monsignor George A. Kelly would seem to agree with this qualified criticism of the Neuhaus thesis. As he recently observed, "The documents of reform and renewal from Rome have never been more numerous or profound, but they do little to regulate latter-day Catholic institutions or Catholic lives at the street level."[20]

Relatedly and unfortunately, Rev. Neuhaus sees himself both somehow and somewhere above the present-day "tired ecclesiastical politics of the last quarter century, the endless wrangling of conservative vs. liberal, progressive vs. traditionalist, liberationist vs. magisterial."[21] As such, he fails to realize that the ushering forth of any Catholic moment requires a great deal of successful (whether tiring or not) "ecclesiastical politics" on the part of conservative, traditional defenders of magisterial authority. The latter are not only, in the main, overwhelmingly far more orthodox than America's "liberal, progressive, and liberationist types" but are far more centrally concerned with restoring the necessary institutional machinery for effective and authentic evangelization efforts. It is clear that Joseph Cardinal Ratzinger understands this far better than does Rev. Neuhaus.

A significant historical aspect of the orthodox Catholic attempt to build social institutions in order to maintain and evangelize the faith entailed the construction of a Catholic educational network from the elementary to the graduate level. The Church's alternative higher education system mirrored secular developments in bureaucratization and professionalization but provided a distinctive and decisive twist through the effort to ground all study through the unifying force of neo-Thomism and neo-Scholasticism with its God-centered teleological focus. Simply put, the Catholic intellectual attempt, in the felicitous phrase of Pope Pius X, was "to restore all things in Christ."[22] (The attempt ultimately failed as the forces of secularization proved greater than those attempting to integrate education under a sacred canopy of Catholic principles.)

Associated with the development of an alternate Catholic educational fortress was the creation of distinctive Catholic social science perspectives and the establishment of separate Catholic scholarly organizations founded on specific premises: that Catholics (1) bring distinctive philosophical/theological presuppositions and metaphysical starting points into their intellectual approaches but (2) should appropriate anything of worth in secular intellectual approaches for the benefit of the faith.[23] As Jeffrey Burns has noted, American Catholic social science initially developed around the turn of the century through the pioneering efforts of the sociologist William Kerby, the economist John A. Ryan, the psychologist Thomas Verner Moore and the anthropologist John M. Cooper.[24] Mention should also be made of the vital role played by the historian Peter Guilday in attempting to counter secular misconceptions and faulty interpretations concerning the history of the Church.[25] David Salvaterra reports that the American Catholic Historical Association was founded in 1919, the Catholic Anthropological Conference and the American Catholic Philosophical Association in 1926, the Catholic Biblical Association of America in 1936, the American Catholic Sociological Society in 1938, the Canon Law Society of America in 1939, the Catholic Economic Association in 1941, the Catholic Theological Society in 1946, the American Catholic Psychological Association in 1947, and the Albertus Magnus Guild, an organization for Catholics in science, in 1953.[26]

In the wake of the Second Vatican Council many of the various Catholic professional associations fell victim either to a "secularization from without," that is, dissolved as specifically "Catholic" organizations or a "secularization from within," that is, internally transformed into shells of their once authentically Catholic selves while still formally keeping the Catholic label. Predictably enough, these secularizing developments—at least according to the subsequent progressivist or Americanist leadership wings of these organizations—were legitimated by Vatican II. The requirements of "ecumenism," "academic freedom," "critical thinking," and "individual conscience" were used to make the case that distinctive Catholic academic perspectives and separate (but, again, not isolated) Catholic professional associations were provincial at best or contradictory at worst. The latent and unintended function of the Council was to permit many Catholic intellectuals to find a too-comfortable home within the frame of reference of the outer secular professional societies. In reality, Vatican II actually affirmed the need for Catholics to engage in public dialogue about what their religion had to offer both to the world at large and to the various intellectual disciplines. Rather than dialoguing with their secular counterparts, many influential post-Vatican II Catholic intellectuals capitulated to their mindset instead. Vatican II was hardly a declaration that distinctive Catholic intellectual approaches and professional associations were obsolescent. In truth it was a call for an open-minded but evangelistic thrust into the temporal sphere of academia and civil society.

Similarly, one can point to yet another case of a "secularization from within" and weakening of a hitherto important set of Catholic institutions, those concerning social welfare. On the one hand, Thomas P. Melady may be factually correct when he asserts that "programs designed to meet social needs are being carried out in every one of our thirty-six Archdioceses and 163 Dioceses in the United States by 1,926 special centers.…[Furthermore]…the services of the American Catholic Church exist to help not only Catholics but persons of all religious affiliations."[27] However, unfortunately, he ignores the crucial reality that most present-day Catholic social service agencies are highly secularized, taking care of bodies but not souls, the material but not the spiritual. This is, predictably enough, the end result of divorcing justice and charity from its necessary doctrinal framework. Ironically, Dr. Melady has ignored this very point, which was made by Pennsylvania senator Rick Santorum, who spoke of the secularization of Catholic institutions at the Annual Convention of the Catholic Campaign for America held on February 20, 1997. As Maggie Gallagher, reflecting on Senator Santorum's speech, states, "the difficult task of helping the poor keep body and soul together in America requires charities that are as vigorously committed to the latter as to the former."[28]

Catholics and Individual Achievement

Third, how successful have Catholic Americans been *individually* (as compared to corporatively)? Individually, contemporary Catholic Americans are quite successful in terms of the sociological dimensions of economic, social, and political attainment *viewed from the frame of reference of secular and materialistic American elites.*

Rev. Andrew M. Greeley's *statistics* (as compared to his typical "Americanist" *interpretation* of his facts), make this clear.[29] Regarding the issue of formal education, Rev. Greeley reports that "Catholics who are maturing in the 1980s are half again as likely to attend college as white Protestants of that same age cohort."[30] He notes the historical comparison of Catholic college attendance rates vis-à-vis white Protestants as follows: from 1910-1929, .7; from 1930-59, .9; from 1960-79, 1.1; and in the mid-1980s, 1.43.[31] Regarding the issue of managerial and professional careers, Rev. Greeley similarly concludes that, as of the mid-1980s, "Catholics are now half again as likely to choose managerial and professional careers as white Protestants."[32] Historically, he presents the Catholic rate vis-à-vis white Protestants as follows: from 1910-19, .65; from 1920-29, .81; from 1930-49, .9; from 1950-59, 1.07; from 1960-79, 1.1; and in the mid-1980s, 1.5.[33] Regarding the issue of income, Rev. Greeley reports that by the early 1980s, Catholics earned more income than white Methodists, white Lutherans, and white Baptists trailing only white Presbyterians, white Episcopalians and Jews.[34] However, he immediately follows, "if one looks at Catholics under forty...one finds...that Catholics...have become the most affluent gentile religious group in America."[35]

Rev. Greeley continues, with his *undefined* sense of just how "successful" are American Catholics in the mid-1980s, by disclosing that there are large numbers of Catholics earning graduate degrees and, furthermore, that Catholics represent between a fifth and a quarter of the professorate, many now found "in the most distinguished universities in the country...and achieving excellence and eminence in these universities."[36] Rev. Greeley concludes, stating that "whatever may have been true of the past, there is no longer any obstacle in the Catholic culture preventing young Catholics from pursuing academic or intellectual or artistic careers and from being as successful as anyone else in these careers."[37] While it is true, as Rev. Greeley notes, that an earlier immigrant and working-class Catholic population understandably had to sacrifice advances in formal education in order to secure financial stability in the family, Rev. Greeley's (again) undefined use of the concept of "Catholic culture" certainly breeds suspicion that he shares the typical—and wrongheaded—Americanist understanding of pre-Vatican II "high culture" as itself anti-intellectual. Furthermore, Rev. Greeley's undefined use of the word "successful," masks, in the post-Vatican II era in the United States, a widespread secularization in the areas of academic, intellectual, professional, artistic, et cetera, life. Whither today, specific Catholic approaches to art, music, and the social sciences? Simply put, American Catholics are overwhelmingly "successful," in both the public and private spheres of society, at being just like those other middle- to upper-middle-class Americans who have abandoned their own religious traditions for the false promises of secular materialism. Rev. Neuhaus is certainly right on the mark when he states that

> the remarkable cultural success of American Catholics in the last half-century is a tragic failure if it means that now Catholics are just like everybody else. Real success is marked by the confidence and courage to challenge the culture of which we are securely part. Or we might put it this way: There is a crucial difference between being American Catholics and being Catholic Americans. We are constantly told that there is a distinctively American way of being Catholic. The course of counter-cultural courage is to demonstrate that there is a distinctively Catholic way of being American. The Catholic Moment happens when American Catholics dare to be Catholic Americans.[38]

In a particularly "loaded" assertion, Rev. Greeley states that "whether it is good or bad to have a well-educated and presumably independent lay population is hardly a matter worth debating; the truth of the matter is that American Catholics have now become well-educated and more independent than Church leadership realizes."[39] The assertion is loaded because Rev. Greeley, again, takes for granted what it means to be "well-educated" and what a true sense of "independence" entails. "Well-educated," for Rev. Greeley, apparently translates into accepting various secular ideologies, fads/foibles included; "independence," for Rev. Greeley (and directly opposed to John Paul II in his *Veritatis Splendor*), apparently means *whatever* one decides *regardless* of the truth and a sound morality. Rev. Greeley ends his chapter on the economic and educational context of Catholic America in the mid-1980s by demonstrating the typical arrogance of a "communal Catholicism" that he has celebrated elsewhere.[40] For Rev. Greeley, "the well-educated Catholic professional is here, he/she is here to stay and is not about to leave the church...[and]...not about to participate in the church on any other terms but his or her own."[41] Given a weak-kneed Catholic ecclesiastical leadership unwilling to exercise its prerogative to excommunicate, or otherwise discipline and instruct the dissident, Rev. Greeley is, sadly, correct in this last assertion.

Regarding the realm of politics, the facts are that Catholic representation in both houses of Congress and among viable presidential candidates has increased significantly since World War II concomitant with the rising educational, occupational, and income of the general Catholic population just discussed. However, Catholics have been anything *but* successful politically, if one defines success in terms of the ability to bring Catholic social thought into the public square from which national social policy is forged. The social scientific evidence is that Catholic politicians have not voted either consistently from a Catholic perspective or as a discernible bloc.

Mary Hanna's analysis is probably the best available in explaining the inability and unwillingness of Catholic politicians to make an impact *qua* Catholic.[42] She notes three reasons. First and foremost, the faith was not a significant factor in the value orientation of many "Catholic" congressmen. Second, even when Congressmen claim a strong allegiance to their faith, internal Catholic pluralism militated against a single vision and concerted activity. As Hanna claims, "there is indeed no one way to be Catholic; it seems clear that the Catholic Church with its rich and complex history, traditions and teachings provides a variety of reference points for its adherents....There is then no single thrust that Catholic religious influence takes in the lives and thinking of the Catholic sector of Congress."[43] Third, Hanna cites "the inhibiting influence of American societal norms stressing Church-State separation and of Congressional norms downplaying representation of any one group and emphasizing the importance of the general or 'public' interest."[44]

Hanna's first explanation provides, sadly, evidence of the fact that the Catholic Church simply has lost the hearts and minds of many of its people through an outright secularization. Hanna's second explanation is more subtle and fascinating. It is indicative of an *internal* secularization that reveals that what is really operant—that what is of *paramount* importance—in the thought and activity of many "Catholic" politicians is some form of non-Catholic allegiance (e.g., socialism, capitalism, feminism, pragmatism, etc.) that selectively chooses what elements of Catholic social doctrine are to be utilized *ideologically*. The Catholic politician, as such, "can have his cake and eat it too," satisfying some non-Catholic ideological interest while simultaneously legitimating his/her action to the Catholic citizenry by clothing it in the trappings of the faith. In responding to Hanna's third explanation, three reactions are in order. The first is to note the false understanding of Church-State separation conveniently assumed by many Catholic politicians. The second is the ignoring, by Catholic politicians, of the natural law tradition accepted by the Church, which claims that its principles are both universal and applicable for the good of all mankind. The third is the blatant "interest group" politics that characterizes much of American political life which, apparently, is acceptable as long as one isn't a Catholic or a member of the so-called "religious right."

Easily the figure in modern American Catholic history that symbolizes worldly political success at the expense of the faith is the one and only American Catholic president, John F. Kennedy, elected in 1960. It is hard to overstate the sense of euphoria that Kennedy's candidacy aroused among many upwardly socially mobile Catholics of the era. Given the historic and rampant anti-Catholicism deeply embedded in American culture, it is easy to understand the emotion aroused when Kennedy finally spiked the ball into the presidential end zone. However, in retrospect, what is historically important about this episode is *not*, as is generally contended, Kennedy's victory per se, but the manner in which he accomplished it. George Gallup, Jr., and Jim Castelli are simply like many typical Americanist spinmasters who purposefully ignore the issue of the secularization of Catholic elites and the Catholic population at large when they disingenuously assert that "the election of John Fitzgerald Kennedy as the first Catholic President of the United States in 1960 was a turning point in American history: with that election, American Catholics came of age politically."[45]

Kennedy's ultimate significance, to the contrary, was to suggest to all aspiring Catholic politicians (or, for that matter, to any Catholic on the make) that no office or honor was beyond reach assuming that one make clear to the non-Catholic world that one's Catholic heritage would be inoperative in any important aspect of public life. Kennedy made this perfectly clear to non-Catholic America in his speech to the Houston Ministerial Alliance during the 1960 national election. Kennedy's political pragmatism has quickly led Catholic politicians down the slippery slope to the more systematized defense of the privatization of the Catholic faith as espoused in the 1980s and 1990s by former New York governor Mario Cuomo.[46]

Unfortunately, the situation regarding the lack of authentic Catholic inspiration for the Catholic laity in American political life is not superior to that of the Catholic politician and, actually, serves the function of "allowing" Catholic politicians to get away with their infidelity to, and ignorance of, the faith. The religious values held by the Catholic lay population vary across the "orthodox-heterodox" spectrum and translate into diverse types of political thought and behavior. While perhaps 10 to 15 percent of the contemporary Catholic population is "orthodox-across-the-board," combining a healthy respect for all aspects of the Catholic faith including, simultaneously, a liturgical and social Catholicism, the rest of Catholic America, unfortunately, must be categorized as different variations of Rev. Greeley's selective or "communal" Catholicism. Communal Catholicism, whether ultimately driven by socialism, capitalism, feminism, new age, or some other non-Catholic ideology, has dramatically and especially increased among the younger cohorts, testimony to the effects of the destruction/weakening of the internal integrity of the "official" organizations of the Catholic Church in the United States. As Stephen M. Krason notes, for the majority of contemporary Catholics, it is some secular form of either liberalism or conservatism that is more centrally important in consciousness than is adherence to the Catholic faith.[47] Krason's analysis suggests "that to promote a social order based on the teachings of the Church and on the natural law, Catholics will have to re-evangelize their own people as well as reach out to other Christians."[48] By implication at least, Krason is informing us that talk of a "Catholic moment" in contemporary American life is premature; Catholic Americans must roll up their sleeves and start the painful process of putting the pieces of their religion back together again in the wake of the post-Vatican II debacle. The Catholic laity, for its part, has hitherto failed in its mission to Christianize the temporal sphere. John Haas's understanding of the specific task of "the lay Christian consecrated through baptism…to bring into the midst of the world the very life of Christ"[49] has gone unfulfilled.

Much of the individual success of Catholics in America, as such, has come at the expense of either abandoning or privatizing the Catholic faith, or in other cases, redefining it to mean something else, as in the case of much of what passes for "liberation theology."[50] Furthermore, such a trade-off was, in many cases, sociologically unnecessary. It was the result of insecure Catholic Americans suffering the social-psychological reality of "resentment," that is, accepting the definitions of reality of one's own anti-Catholic oppressors, rather than out of any (alleged) *intrinsic* requirement to abandon the faith (e.g., in order to become a scientist or sociologist) or *extrinsic* political or status consideration (e.g., in order to move into the cultural center).

Whether sociologically necessary or not, such an abandonment/weakening constitutes a serious theological offense against a Catholic religion positing that the ultimate goal of all individuals is, paraphrasing Saint Augustine, to have one's soul rest with the Lord in Heaven. The common folk wisdom that "all that glitters is not gold" is perfected in the rhetorical question asked in the Bible, that is, "What does it profit a man to gain the whole world but lose his soul?" (Mt. 16:26)

Notes

1.   George Gallup, Jr., and Jim Castelli, *The American Catholic People: Their Beliefs, Practices, and Values* (New York: Doubleday, 1987), 187.
2.   Gallup and Castelli, *The American Catholic People*, 6.
3.   Gallup and Castelli, *The American Catholic People*, 51.
4.   Pope John Paul II, "Sollicitudo Rei Socialis, #21," in *Aspiring to Freedom: Commentaries on John Paul II's Encyclical, The Social Concerns of the Church*, Kenneth A. Meyers, ed. (Grand Rapids, Michigan: Eerdmans, 1988), 23.
5.   Rev. Andrew M. Greeley, *The Catholic Myth: The Behavior and Beliefs of American Catholics* (New York: Charles Scribner's Sons, 1990), 300.
6.   Peter L. Berger, *Pyramids of Sacrifice: Political Ethics and Social Change* (New York: Basic Books, 1974). For a more obviously sympathetic reading of democratic capitalism, see Berger's *The Capitalist Revolution: Fifty Propositions about Prosperity, Equality, and Liberty* (New York: Basic Books, 1986).
7.   Joseph A. Varacalli, *The Catholic and Politics in Post-World War II America: A Sociological Analysis* (St. Louis, Missouri: Society of Catholic Social Scientists, 1995), 19-20.

8. Michael Novak, *The Spirit of Democratic Capitalism* (New York: Simon and Schuster, 1982).

9. Thomas A. Droleskey, "Buchanan Says He Is Only Prolife Candidate Who Can Win Nomination," *The Wanderer* (8 February 1996): 5. David J. Peterson, "Should America Examine the Morality of Free Trade?" *The Wanderer* (8 February 1996): 6.

10. Charles E. Rice, "Why Pat Should Go," *The Wanderer* (25 April 1996): 6-7.

11. American Catholic Lawyers Association, "Do Pat Buchanan's Views Contradict Catholic Teaching?" *The Wanderer* (21 March 1996): 12.

12. Joseph A. Varacalli, "Divided We Fall, Unwelcome Conclusions: Review Essay on Peter Brimelow's *Alien Nation: Common Sense about America's Immigration Disaster*," *Crisis* 13, no. 10 (November 1995): 48-49.

13. Greeley, *The Catholic Myth*, 290.

14. Gallup and Castelli, *The American Catholic People*, 7.

15. Rev. Richard J. Neuhaus, *The Catholic Moment: The Paradox of the Church in the Postmodern World* (San Francisco, California: Harper and Row, 1987). Rev. Richard J. Neuhaus, "The Catholic Moment in America," in *Catholics in the Public Square: The Role of Catholics in American Life, Culture, and Politics*, Thomas P. Melady, ed. (Huntington, Indiana: Our Sunday Visitor, 1995).

16. Neuhaus, *The Catholic Moment*, 283.

17. Neuhaus, "The Catholic Moment in America," 28.

18. Rev. Andrew M. Greeley, *The Catholic Experience* (New York: Doubleday, 1967).

19. Dennis P. McCann, *New Experiment in Democracy: The Challenge for American Catholicism* (Kansas City, Missouri: Sheed and Ward, 1987).

20. Monsignor George A. Kelly, *The Battle for the American Church Revisited* (San Francisco, California: Ignatius Press, 1995), 11.

21. Neuhaus, "The Catholic Moment in America," 37.

22. David L. Salvaterra, *American Catholicism and the Intellectual Life* (New York: Garland Press, 1988), 201.

23. Joseph A. Varacalli, "Renewing the Battle to Restore Sociology and the Social Sciences in Christ," *Fellowship of Catholic Scholars Newsletter* 14, no. 2 (June 1991): 21-24. Joseph A. Varacalli, "The Society of Catholic Social Scientists: Catholic Social Science and the Reconstruction of the Social Order," *Faith and Reason* 22, nos. 1-2 (spring-summer 1996): 3-14.

24. Jeffrey Burns, *American Catholics and the Family Crisis, 1930-1962: An Ideological and Organizational Response* (New York: Garland Press, 1988), 10.

25. Salvaterra, *American Catholicism and the Intellectual Life*, 237.

26. Salvaterra, *American Catholicism and the Intellectual Life*, 79-80.

27. Thomas P. Melady, "From a Lonely Minority to a Strong Presence," in *Public Catholicism: The Challenge of Living the Faith in a Secular Culture*, Thomas P. Melady, ed. (Huntington, Indiana: Our Sunday Visitor, 1996), 14.

28. Maggie Gallagher, "Catholic Charity, But Keep It Quiet," *New York Post* (2 June 1997): 21.

29. Rev. Andrew M. Greeley, *American Catholics Since the Council: An Unauthorized Report* (Chicago, Illinois: Thomas More Press, 1985).

30. Greeley, *American Catholics Since the Council*, 27.

31. Greeley, *American Catholics Since the Council*, 27.

32. Greeley, *American Catholics Since the Council*, 28.

33.   Greeley, *American Catholics Since the Council,* 27-28.
34.   *Greeley, American Catholics Since the Council,* 29.
35.   Greeley, *American Catholics Since the Council,* 29-30.
36.   Greeley, *American Catholics Since the Council,* 31-32.
37.   Greeley, *American Catholics Since the Council,* 31.
38.   Neuhaus, "The Catholic Moment in America," 35.
39.   Greeley, *American Catholics Since the Council,* 33.
40.   Rev. Andrew M. Greeley, *The American Catholic* (New York: Basic Books, 1977). Rev. Andrew M. Greeley, *The Communal Catholic* (New York: Seabury Press, 1976).
41.   Greeley, *American Catholics Since the Council,* 34.
42.   Mary Hanna, *Catholics and American Politics* (Cambridge, Massachusetts: Harvard University Press, 1979).
43.   Hanna, *Catholics and American Politics,* 86-87.
44.   Hanna, *Catholics and American Politics,* 100.
45.   Gallup and Castelli, *The American Catholic People,* 1.
46.   Varacalli, *The Catholic and Politics in Post-World War II America,* 37-38.
47.   Stephen M. Krason, *Liberalism, Conservatism, and Catholicism: An Evaluation of Contemporary American Political Ideologies in Light of Catholic Social Teaching* (New Hope, Kentucky: Catholics United for the Faith, 1991).
48.   Krason, *Liberalism, Conservatism, and Catholicism,* 258.
49.   John M. Haas, "The Call of the Second Vatican Council to the Laity," in *Catholics in the Public Square,* Thomas Patrick Melady, ed. (Huntington, Indiana: Our Sunday Visitor, 1995), 52.
50.   Joseph A. Varacalli, "A Catholic Sociological Critique of Gustavo Gutierrez's *A Theology of Liberation," Catholic Social Science Review* 1 (1996): 175-189.

Chapter Two

The Discrediting and Unraveling of the Contemporary American Public Order

All indications are that an increasingly larger percentage of American citizens have little confidence in the performance of America's public sphere institutions and in the moral character of the latter's leaders. As sociologist David Poponoe, for one, bluntly admits, "More people are viewing our once accepted social institutions with considerable skepticism. As measured by public opinion polls, confidence in such public institutions as medicine, higher education, the law, the press, and organized religion has declined dramatically."[1] This distrust and cynicism is largely justified and can be explained primarily by two developments, one structural and one cultural-moral.

Structurally, American society has been witnessing, over the past century, a movement toward bigness, abstractness, impersonality, bureaucratization and a concentration of power in its public sphere institutions.[2] This movement progressively "frees" the leaders of these institutions from the direct and even indirect accountability to a concerned citizenry. As the classical sociologist, Max Weber, so astutely observed in his analysis of American community life during the turn of the last century, "according to all experience there is no stronger means of breeding traits than through the necessity of holding one's own in the circle of one's associates."[3] Put into the more exhaustive conceptual framework of sociologist Edward Shils, one can state that "personal," "primordial," and "sacred" ties are, at least for the average individual, more effective in holding human activity accountable than are "civil" allegiances.[4] Put yet another way, given the human tendency to fall toward sin, in the absence of a strong sacramental life and without local community pressure to conduct one's daily activities within moral boundaries, ever more "autonomous" institutions and institutional leaders act, more and more, out of self-centered naked interest that eventually leads to simple corruption.

Culturally-morally, America's elite leaders have progressively abandoned a common Judaic-Christian religious heritage in favor of some secular alternative. As A. James Reichley, among many others, has persuasively argued, even high-minded secular civil humanistic ideologies will eventually succumb to hypocrisy, self-contradiction, and corruption.[5] If God is perceived as dead, following a Nietzsche-like logic, then anything is—or will eventually be seen as—possible. Speaking of the two forms of civil humanism spawned by the Enlightenment—the first drawing on the libertarian side descended from Locke by way of the British utilitarians and the second drawing on the communitarian side descended from Rousseau by way of Hegel and Marx—Reichley concludes that

> both lines of argument have propagated distinguished bodies of social philosophy and have influenced the formation of social institutions and political behavior. Neither, however, has fully escaped the bias toward destructive tendencies that tainted it at the start: among the libertarians tendencies toward atomistic selfishness, obsessive materialism, and personal alienation, and among the communitarians toward social indoctrination, state control, and group aggression.[6]

Put another way, only an awareness of the transcendent God of the Biblical orbit is capable of providing the necessary rock and universal standard for sustaining ethical behavior over the long run. As Reichley puts it so well, only "theist-humanism solves the problem of balancing individual rights against social authority by rooting both in God's transcendent purpose, which is concerned for the welfare of each human soul."[7]

Habits of the Heart: Individualism and Commitment in American Life is an important sociological analysis of changing cultural developments in American society that is crucially informed by the liberal Protestant perspective of its lead coauthor, Robert N. Bellah.[8] In this analysis, Bellah and his colleagues express the concern that modern day American individualism "may have grown cancerous—that it may be destroying those social integuments that Tocqueville saw as moderating its more destructive potentialities.... We are also interested in those cultural traditions and practices that, without destroying individuality, serve to limit and restrain the destructive side of individualism and provide alternative models of how Americans might live."[9] Catholic political scientist Stephen M. Krason's claim[10] that Catholic social teaching is one of the best kept secrets in America is undoubtedly true; in this much celebrated volume Bellah and associates show no indication that the cultural tradition they are looking for is a Catholic social thought that includes within its conceptual corpus such vital and true principles as personalism, solidarity, and subsidiarity and that can replace such principles as, respectively, individualism, totalism, and statism.[11]

The solution for America's ever increasing and ever more serious set of social pathologies (e.g., abortion, crime, divorce, single-parent families, teenage suicide and pregnancy, drug addiction, welfarism, abortion, AIDS, etc.) as discussed by William J. Bennett,[12] among many others, lies not primarily in technical expertise but in the development and institutionalization of a Catholic informed morality. A large percentage of the Catholic population at large—again, admittedly including many Catholics in name only—is either ignorant of the social doctrine of the Church or in fundamental disagreement with this claim. According to Gallup and Castelli's research, "in 1957, 83 percent of both Catholics and Protestants said religion could answer all or most of the day's problems. In 1985, the number of Protestants answering in the affirmative had fallen to 70 percent, while the response among Catholics had declined to only 52 percent."[13]

Until God is brought back centrally in the equations of the American public order, it will continue to unravel and become ever more discredited. While God's patience may be, theologically speaking, infinite, it is theologically wrong to *presuppose* his continued mercy. And, from a secular historical viewpoint, simply put, civilizations rise and fall. American civilization may be much more "on the ropes" than many suspect. As Michael Novak has put it:

> we have reason to fear for the future of this Republic. And fear for it, precisely, on moral and intellectual grounds. Intellectually, morally, our nation is on the wrong track. On our campuses, in our movie industry, on our television talk shows and sitcoms, in our law schools, in our courts, in our newspapers and newsweeklies, in our gay bars and our frenetically busy abortion clinics (slicing to death or killing with acid 1.5 million helpless citizens per year) we have witnessed an aggressive hostility to Judaism and Christianity—to any source of transcendent judgment—a hostility unprecedented in our national experience.[14]

Novak, however, (1) tends to restrict his understanding of the contemporary intellectual and moral rot to only the public sphere of American life and (2) fails to understand that this rot is the inevitable result of the limitations inherent in a social order based on liberalism. As he states, "what is dismaying in America today is not the private striving and private virtue of ordinary mothers and fathers of families, grandparents, uncles and aunts and cousins. It is the corrupt *public ethos*—the public ecology—that is poisoning our public spaces."[15] Unfortunately as I see it, Novak understates the extent of the problem. While Novak correctly understands that the poison emanates from our contemporary secular naked square, he fails to fully appreciate how widespread many in the middle, especially upper-middle, class have imbibed of the poison. This is especially important given that the middle class has historically been the important base for social change in American society. He also understates how necessarily "radical" is the solution to the decaying American social order. Novak fails to see that the only long term solution is an American civilization based on the social doctrine of the Catholic Church.

Notes

1. David Poponoe, "The American Family Crisis," in *Taking Sides: Clashing Views on Controversial Issues*, 9th ed., Kurt Finsterbusch and George McKenna, eds. (Guilford, Connecticut: Duskin, 1996), 117.

2. Peter L. Berger and Richard J. Neuhaus, *To Empower People: The Role of Mediating Structures in Public Policy* (Washington, D.C.: American Enterprise Institute, 1977).

3. Max Weber, *From Max Weber*, Hans C. Gerth and C. Wright Mills, eds. (New York: Oxford University Press, 1946), 320.

4. Edward A. Shils, "Primordial, Personal, Sacred, and Civil Ties," in *Center and Periphery: Essays in Macro Sociology*, Edward A. Shils, ed. (Chicago: University of Chicago Press, 1975).

5. A. James Reichley, *Religion in American Public Life* (Washington, D.C.: Brookings Institution, 1985).

6. Reichley, *Religion in American Public Life*, 344-345.

7. Reichley, *Religion in American Public Life*, 52.

8. Robert N. Bellah et al., *Habits of the Heart: Individualism and Commitment in American Life* (New York: Harper and Row, 1985).

9. Bellah et al., *Habits of the Heart*, viii.

10. Stephen M. Krason, et al., *Liberalism, Conservatism, and Catholicism: An Evaluation of Contemporary American Political Ideologies in Light of Catholic Social Teaching* (New Hope, Kentucky: Catholics United for the Faith, 1991).

11. However, in fairness it should be noted that Bellah and his colleagues do mention some of the tenets of social Catholicism in their follow-up volume, published six years later. See Robert N. Bellah et al., *The Good Society* (New York: Alfred A. Knopf, 1991).

12. William J. Bennett, *The Index of Leading Cultural Indicators* (Washington, D.C.: Heritage Foundation, 1993).

13. George Gallup, Jr., and Jim Castelli, *The American Catholic People: Their Beliefs, Practices, and Values* (Garden City, New York: Doubleday, 1987), 12.

14. Michael Novak, "The Rediscovery of Our American Catholic Heritage" in *Catholics in the Public Square*, Thomas Patrick Melady, ed. (Huntington, Indiana: Our Sunday Visitor, 1995), 148.

15. Novak, "The Rediscovery of Our American Catholic Heritage," 148.

Chapter Three

The Pyrrhic Victory of Liberalism:
The Exhaustion of an Inadequate Idea

Following the analysis of Robert Bellah and his associates, the key American value has historically been that of individualism.[1] The nature and carrier of individualism has changed, however, during the lifespan of the American nation. Originally, during the colonial era, individualism was both contained and given direction toward public life and service by either certain forms of Protestantism, especially by the theocratic impulse found in early Calvinism, or by an Enlightenment deism. Bellah and his coauthors have referred to these as, respectively, *biblical* and *republican* forms of individualism.[2] With the establishment of both corporate capitalism and the subjectivism often associated with the processes of modernity, individualism has seen itself progressively freed from *any* public orientation, focusing instead either on the narrow demands of one's occupation or the search for privatized meaning and the pursuit of self-centered happiness. Bellah and his associates have referred to these present realities of American life as, respectively, *utilitarian* and *expressive* forms of individualism.[3] As Bellah and his coauthors state, "it took the geographic and economic expansion of the new nation, especially in the years after 1800, to produce the restless quest for material betterment...[in which modern forms of] individualism...develop their own inherent tendencies in relative independence from civic and religious forms of life."[4]

A somewhat similar case has been made by Daniel Bell.[5] Bell argues that the realms of culture and economics have long since been emancipated from the influence of what Peter L. Berger[6] would call a religiously informed societal "sacred canopy." Furthermore, for Bell, both the *cultural drive of modernity* and the *capitalist economic impulse*, while now sharing a common origin in the rejection both of tradition and in the authority of everything past, stand in an adversarial relationship to each other. Bell additionally argues that, today, the cultural realm of modernity has emerged victorious. Put another way, the norms of work, delayed gratification, career orientation, and devotion to enterprise have succumbed to the unbridled quest for the enhancement of the self, at least for the American middle class. Translated into Bellah's framework, *expressive individualism* has trumped *utilitarian individualism*. Put into a Catholic restorationist critique, the self-liquidating nature of an American civilization ultimately based on the cultural value of individualism is approaching its logical end of the road, that is, the absurdity contained within the idea of what David Riesman, Nathan Glazer, and Reuel Denny among others, have termed an "autonomous individualism."[7]

The selfish, inward side of the individualism at the heart of the American founding was also probably both contained and given centrifugal direction toward service to the public order by the acceptance, consciously held or not, of natural law thinking with its positing of the existence of an objective moral order. However, this natural law thinking was not only shaped by a Catholic matrix of ideas and sentiments forged during the Middle Ages but also by the pagan and neo-pagan traditions, respectively, of ancient Greece/Rome and the Enlightenment. This diluted natural law thinking was, furthermore, less than satisfactorily carried out in the colonies by either the aforementioned biblical individualism or republican individualism, both with their own self-liquidating and internally contradictory impulses. Donald J. D'Elia, for one, has analyzed the relativism lurking within the thought of Thomas Jefferson and the inauthentic Christianity of some of the other American Founding Fathers.[8] Some features of early American history—including the genocide of the native Indian populations, the peculiarly harsh treatment of blacks in the southern slavery system, and the exploitation of workers of a laissez-faire capitalism—are testimony to the less than fully effective mediation of the universal truths commonly held in the early Republic. Natural law thinking was probably most effectively institutionalized in American society during the early to mid-twentieth century as the Catholic Church was at the height of its institutional integrity and starting to exert, for the first time, a certain amount of cultural influence.[9] John Courtney Murray's thesis[10] about the formative role of natural law thinking on the Republic, relatively speaking, makes sense more in the context of when it was authored, that is, in the late 1950s, and less as a statement of historical reality during the colonial period. (My argument, then, positions me between the thought of those like Russell Kirk[11] who accepts the idea that the "roots of the American order" were based on the natural law and those "communitarians" like Benjamin Barber[12] who hold that America has historically never embraced any public purpose, is radically pluralistic, and is held together by proceduralism and the adversarial method.) Superseding an original Protestant cultural hegemony, Catholicism played a not insignificant role in the formation of a common unifying Judaic-Christian heritage strongest in immediate post-World War II America, which now has itself been replaced by a secular monopoly in the American public square.

The early forms of American individualism that seemed to be in the process of being morally strengthened by, relatively speaking, a stronger Catholic presence in mid-twentieth century American society, have now turned against themselves without any effective support from Protestant, humanistic, or Catholic sources. Natural law thinking was transformed into either natural rights thinking or positivism, which turned out to be little more than temporary "way stations" for contemporary various subjectivist absurdities like atheistic existentialist and deconstructionist outlooks. Ralph McInerny discusses this movement in philosophical approaches as one from the "classical" to the "modern": "the classical view requires that every discussion, every truth claim, be such that we can be led back from it to those great common truths which everybody knows and which are the ultimate warrant for accepting whatever be proposed. Modernity begins with the denial that there is such a fund of commonly possessed non-gainsayable truths to which reference must always be made."[13] The irony, in the case of Catholicism, is that there are no contradictions internal to its own ideational system. Catholicism, as I will subsequently argue, constitutes an eternal balancing act between sets of dyadic opposites that, in its totality, provides for the full spectrum of healthy human experience and presents the proper relations between mind, body, society, and cosmos.[14] The damage done to Catholicism as the carrier of the natural law was not inevitable but needlessly self-inflicted by its own leaders in their attempt to gain acceptance by conforming to the currently fashionable. These self-inflicted wounds run the gamut from the obvious to the somewhat more subtle: from the Catholic professor's reduction of the social doctrine of the Church into a Marxist inspired theology of liberation, from the parish priest denying the objective reality of sin in the confessional to his constant reference to the "human side" of Jesus in homilies, from the Bishop's tacit allowance to have a Dignity Mass run in his diocese to the marriage tribunal's misuse of psychological grounds in granting annulments.

Today one witnesses an American society without an effective and moral guiding public theology/philosophy and a prevalent run amok individualism seeking short term material success and hedonistic pleasure. Socialism caters to the elite and selfish interests and worldview of the "new knowledge class" and capitalism caters to the equally elite and selfish interests and worldview of the "old business class." The casualties are a lack of any effective concern for the common good and for the fundamental dignity of each and every person and, even more importantly, the risk of imperiling the salvation of millions of individual souls.

"My own conclusion is very clear," writes philosopher Alasdair MacIntyre. "It is that on the one hand we still, in spite of the efforts of three centuries of moral philosophy and one of sociology, lack any coherent rationally defensible statement of a liberal individualist point of view; and that, on the other hand, the Aristotelian tradition can be restated in a way that restores intelligibility and rationality to our moral and social attitudes and commitments."[15] The "restatement of the Aristotelian tradition," I argue, must be found in an updated synthesis of faith and reason in the Thomistic tradition, which forms the basis for the social doctrine of the Church. As of now, unfortunately, the social doctrine of the Church remains untapped, an unrecognized buried treasure.

Historian Philip Gleason reminds us of the sentiments of many Catholics in the era between the two world wars: "True social reform, as Catholics understood it...required displacement of liberal individualism and the restoration of a communal order characterized by organic unity and solidarity."[16] He ends his volume, *Keeping the Faith*, on what is hopefully a prophetic note. Regarding the glorious attempt of the preconciliar Catholic leadership to "restore all things in Christ" through their promotion of integrating visions, an organic Catholic culture, and the synthesis of natural and supernatural truth, Gleason implores that "we should honor their attempt, try to understand it, and endeavor to profit from it."[17]

Notes

1.   Robert N. Bellah et al., *Habits of the Heart: Individualism and Commitment in American Life* (New York: Harper and Row, 1985).
2.   Bellah et al., *Habits of the Heart*.
3.   Bellah et al., *Habits of the Heart*.
4.   Bellah et al., *Habits of the Heart*, 147.
5.   Daniel Bell, *The Cultural Contradictions of Capitalism* (New York: Basic Books, 1976).
6.   Peter L. Berger, *The Sacred Canopy: Elements of a Sociological Theory of Religion* (Garden City, New York: Doubleday and Company, 1967).
7.   David Riesman, Nathan Glazer, and Reuel Denny, *The Lonely Crowd: A Study of the Changing American Character* (New Haven, Connecticut: Yale University Press, 1961).
8.   Donald J. D'Elia, *The Spirits of '76: A Catholic Inquiry* (Front Royal, Virginia: Christendom Press, 1983).
9.   Joseph A. Varacalli, "The Contemporary Culture War in America: Whither Natural Law, Catholic Style?" *Faith and Reason* 21, no. 4 (winter 1995): 355-371.
10.   Rev. John Courtney Murray, *We Hold These Truths: Catholic Reflections on the American Proposition* (New York: Image Books, 1964). Donald J. D'Elia and Stephen M. Krason, Introduction, in *We Hold These Truths and More: Further Catholic Reflections on the American Proposition*, Donald J. D'Elia and Stephen M. Krason, eds. (Steubenville, Ohio: Franciscan University, 1993).
11.   Russell Kirk, *The Roots of the American Order* (LaSalle, Illinois: Open Court Publishing, 1974).
12.   Benjamin Barber, "The Compromised Republic: Public Purposelessness in America," in *The Moral Foundations of the American Republic*, Robert H. Horwitz, ed. (Charlottesville, Virginia: University of Virginia Press, 1977).

13. Ralph McInerny, *A First Glance at St. Thomas Aquinas: A Handbook for Peeping Thomists* (Notre Dame, Indiana: University of Notre Dame Press, 1990), 59.

14. See chapter 7 of this volume, "Catholic Philosophical Vision, Catholic Historical Reality: The Need for a Catholic Plausibility Structure."

15. Alasdair MacIntyre, *After Virtue: A Study in Moral Theory* (Notre Dame, Indiana: University of Notre Dame Press, 1984), 259.

16. Philip Gleason, *Keeping the Faith: American Catholicism Past and Present* (Notre Dame, Indiana: University of Notre Dame Press, 1987), 141.

17. Gleason, *Keeping the Faith*, 151.

Chapter Four

The American Culture War and the Civil War within the Catholic Church of the United States

As James Hunter, among many others, has persuasively argued, American civilization is presently in the midst of a full-blown cultural war.[1] The war plays itself out across a broad spectrum of American social institutions: the family, education, media and the arts, law, and electoral politics, among others. Furthermore, the battle is not just between groups and personalities but, more importantly, between highly articulated moral visions and worldviews.

One warring faction is an upper-middle to middle-class "new knowledge class" composed of secular and progressive intellectuals, social activists, bureaucrats, therapists of one sort or another, complete with the target populations that justify their philosophies and social programs, that is, specifically, and somewhat arbitrarily, designated "victims of injustice"/"minority groups." On the other side of the barricades are to be found the lower-middle class to middle-class orthodox remnants of a once, but no longer, dominant Judaic-Christian heritage. With the qualified exception of its Catholic component, this coalition tends to be ideologically procapitalist or, at the very least, tolerant of capitalism. Put another way, for practical purposes, American society is no longer characterized and unified by one dominant overarching "collective conscience" in the Durkheimian sense[2] but by two almost diametrically opposed moralities. This is but one consequence of the abandonment of the natural law in American life;[3] Glenn N. Schram for one, has recently made the case for the development of a "New American Civil Theology" based on natural law foundations.[4]

It is, of course, the case that not all of America fits neatly into one or the other camp in the cultural war. Many Americans, on an individual basis, take logically contradictory positions on specific issues or are either confused or ambivalent about where they stand in this war.[5] Not a few Americans, for instance, are "privately" on the side of the Judaic-Christian heritage but have accepted "publicly" the philosophy of moral relativism as a way to "get along with" one's neighbors.[6] Or, in other cases, in order to avoid social and political persecution, they refuse to "offer offense"[7] to ideological positions they realize are wrongheaded. Many Americans, furthermore, take their positions on the issues of the cultural war not based on well thought out theological or philosophical reasoning but rather on subjective sentiment and emotion thus betraying the general societal movement away from reliance on both reason and an objective moral order. Referring to the work of John Henry Cardinal Newman, Robert George has identified a counterfeit form of conscience based on "self-will." As George puts it, "Conscience as what Newman called 'self-will' is a matter of emotion, not reason. It is concerned not with the identification of what one has a duty to do or not to do, one's feelings to the contrary notwithstanding, but rather, and precisely, with sorting out one's feelings. Conscience as 'self-will' identifies permissions, not obligations."[8]

In yet other cases, certain sectors of the American population structurally do not fit in neatly with either side of the conflict. The populist working classes seem, for instance, to be somewhat culturally (not religiously) close to the Judaic-Christian orthodox coalition but, given their economically precarious position, are attracted to, or at least don't want to fully abandon, the quasi-socialist policies of the new class. Many unionists, for instance, exhibit a stubborn unwillingness to give a hearing to new populist political leaders like Pat Buchanan who refuse to defend—hook, line, and sinker—narrowly defined union interests. The upper "old business class," on the other hand, while recognizing new class thought and programs as often antithetical to capitalism, nonetheless is more and more in line with the new class in its acceptance of a libertine and "emancipated" personal morality.

Theoretically, this ongoing cultural war should not affect the integrity of the Catholic Church and the thought and practice of its millions of adherents. Theoretically, the accumulated and rich doctrine, including social doctrine, of the Church should place Catholicism as a distinct third entity, being isomorphic with neither contending party in the culture war, although sharing, relatively speaking, more overlap with the orthodox Judaic-Christian alliance. However, given the inability of the Church's leaders in America to keep its house together by effectively transmitting and evangelizing the Catholic worldview, external ideologies (e.g., feminist, socialist, capitalist, therapeutic, new age, homosexual, etc.) have made strong internal inroads into the Church, both structurally and attitudinally, thus polarizing and factionalizing the Mystical Body of Christ. The Catholic Church in the United States, given a false legitimacy by the misuse of the concept of individual conscience,[9] is today characterized by divergent interest groups that range from hardened feminists to capitalist-promoting neoconservatives to revolutionary Marxists to self-absorbed new agers to romantic medievalists.

Archbishop Fulton Sheen, in this regard, was right on the mark when he observed:

> When the Church is holy—that is to say, when we the membership of the Church are holy...the opposition always comes from outside the Church—for example, in persecution. When the Church is not so holy, as it is now, then the opposition comes from within—from his [the Pope's] own. That is why he [Pope Paul VI] said his heart was broken.[10]

The classic text on the internal splintering of the Catholic Church in the United States is Monsignor George A. Kelly's *The Battle for the American Church* written in 1979. As Monsignor Kelly put it:

> Vatican II put an end to Catholic serenity. Organized factionalism came quickly, customarily identified by the usual political labels—"left" or "right." These categories are somewhat unfair to all parties, if only because on any given issue convictions and loyalties shift. However, those who placed high value on the security of the Church were distinguishable from those who wanted all possible accommodation with the secular world if you will. For want of a better terminology, *ecclesialists* and *modernizers* marshaled troops according to their cherished priorities....*Ecclesialists* tend to accept established Church positions, a nature of things ordained by God, the necessity of formulas to embody for men what God has revealed, the unique position of the Church as the Body of Christ, the authoritative role of bishops and Pope in defining Catholic faith and morals, and the obligation of obedience to the Church's major directives, which bind all who profess the Catholic faith. *Modernizers*, on the other hand, believe that God is as much moving through the world (immanence) as he is in heaven (transcendence). Divine revelation, therefore, is ongoing, not merely "a deposit of faith," a revelation about a Person, not so much a body of ideas. The modernizer stresses the evolving nature of man's understanding of God's purposes, the importance of personal human experience to that understanding, the voice of believers as important as the voice of hierarchy. In this view, pilgrim people need flexibility in choosing their answers to religious questions, and no prefixed solutions to human problems.[11]

Monsignor Kelly then demonstrates how the *ecclesialist-modernizer* dichotomy usefully explains the intra-Church controversies over the nature of the Church, the renewal of religious life, divine revelation, religious freedom in the Church, doctrinal issues like contraception, and the extent and nature of Church involvement in worldly affairs. Writing fifteen years later in his revised version of *Battle*, Monsignor Kelly indicates some of the dysfunctional consequences resulting from the takeover of large sectors of the Catholic Church in America by the modernizers. He lists ten:

(1) The Church, whose fundamental function is the worship of God in the Eucharist, suffered a severe decrease in Sunday Mass attendance, from the highest in the non-Catholic world to levels more in common with the less-practicing populations in Europe.

(2)The Church, which once averaged three priests for each of her eighteen thousand parishes, most of them young to middle-age and American born, suffered flight from the priesthood and religious life to an alarming extent.

(3)Many dioceses began to be financially strapped; some verged on bankruptcy.

(4)The largest Catholic school system in the world fell into rapid decline, feeding a growing suspicion that (at the elementary and high school levels) it will be virtually extinct sometime in the twenty-first century.

(5)Those who can afford to pay high tuition rates, or who are subsidized, will still enter Catholic schools, but the purpose for which these schools were created a century ago will have been vitiated.

(6)The only form of education still bearing the name Catholic that is now growing numerically is the college system, but for all practical purposes it now places higher value on its secular service than on its religious reason for existence.

(7)The results of a remarkable array of opinion studies indicate that (a) Catholic youth are so badly trained under Catholic auspices that they are called "religious illiterates"; and (b) their parents, although the majority are still church-goers, now think like non-Catholics and are often praised in enlightened circles for a "pick and choose" Catholicity.

(8)The Catholic hierarchy, presiding officers in a sacramental Church, encounter problems today never faced by their predecessors, at least in this century: high rates of premarital copulation, lower rates of valid marriage and infant births, increased divorces on a par with other Americans, widespread use of contraception and/or sterilization, even among church-goers, general acceptance of abortion in special circumstances, a high enough rate of diocesan-approved annulments to create the impression that marriage for Catholics is no longer necessarily indissoluble. (Sixty thousand annulments annually, 80 percent of the Church's world total, do not offer evidence at the parish level of Vatican II's call for holiness as the chief mark of ecclesial reform.)

(9)The Church which, following Christ, taught that deadly sin is the most serious obex to her people's happiness here, and to salvation hereafter, and must be submitted by Christ's will to a penitential process, has within a quarter-century experienced the virtual disappearance of the sacrament of Penance. Furthermore, Church leaders seem unable to reinstitute its common use.

(10) The most sacred of all sacraments, the Eucharist, repository of Christ's living Body, whose reception was intended by him to be the Church's simplest indication of personal and ecclesial holiness, is now widely received by many who are living in serious sin. Certain theologians, and a few bishops, ignore the practice of unworthy reception, condemned today by John Paul II as it was by St. Paul in the beginning.[12]

To date, unfortunately, the winning progressivist secular worldview in the broader culture war has been passively absorbed by the winning liberal

Americanist side in the battle for the American Church although, it must be added, the spectrum of religious heterodoxy from an authentic Catholicism in America contains more than that of the dominant left wing Americanist option. Other forms of heterodoxy include some "right wing" Americanists attempting to cut the Catholic faith down to the contours of our prevailing system of democratic capitalism and the small remnant of pre-Vatican II traditionalists who refuse to accept the authenticity and validity of the Second Vatican Council. These "traditionalists" run the spectrum from those who oppose the liturgical changes brought about in the name of the Council to those who claim that the See of Peter has actually been "vacant" ("sede vacantist") since the end of the pontificate of Pope Pius XII. That the former "right wing Americanists" constitute but another variation of Enlightenment thinking is obvious. Less obvious but nonetheless a reality is that some pre-Vatican II traditionalists are also modernizers in the sense that they—in typically "modern" fashion—are audacious enough to claim to decide for themselves what is the authentic Catholic tradition. All of this is further sad testimony to the sociological fact that the contemporary Catholic Church has been excessively shaped by American social forces to the point of being incapable of shaping, in any significant way, the American Republic.

Notes

1.   James D. Hunter, *Culture Wars: The Struggle to Define America* (New York: Basic Books, 1991). James D. Hunter, *Before the Shooting Begins: Searching for Democracy in America's Culture War* (New York: Free Press, 1994).

2.   Emile Durkheim, *The Elementary Forms of the Religious Life* (New York: Collier Books, 1965).

3.   Joseph A. Varacalli, "The Contemporary Culture War in America: Whither Natural Law, Catholic Style?" *Faith and Reason* 21, no. 4 (winter 1995): 355-371.

4.   Glenn N. Schram, "Toward a New American Civil Theology," *The Wanderer* (6 June 1996): 7.

5.   Hunter, *Culture Wars.* Hunter, *Before the Shooting Begins.*

6.   Allan Bloom, *The Closing of the American Mind* (New York: Simon and Schuster, 1987).

7.   John Cuddihy, *No Offense: Civil Religion and Protestant Taste* (New York: Seabury, 1978).

8.   Robert George, "Catholic Conscience and the Law," in *Catholics in the Public Square*, Thomas Patrick Melady, ed. (Huntington, Indiana: Our Sunday Visitor, 1995), 106.

9.   Joseph A. Varacalli, "Review of Patrick H. McNamara's *Conscience First, Tradition Second: A Story of Young American Catholics*," *Sociological Analysis* 53, no. 4 (winter 1992): 458-460.

10.   Gerard Morrissey, *The Crisis of Dissent* (Front Royal, Virginia: Christendom College Press, 1985), 12.

11.   Monsignor George A. Kelly, *The Battle for the American Church* (New York: Doubleday, 1979), 15-16.

12.   Monsignor George A. Kelly, *The Battle for the American Church Revisited* (San Francisco, California: Ignatius Press, 1995), 21-23.

Chapter Five

Not Enough: The Insufficiency of Evangelical Protestantism

Originally generically Protestant in the early twentieth century, America's central value system moved, first, into a common Judaic-Christian framework and, from the 1960s onwards, into one more purely secular in nature. As many scholars have noted, Protestantism, or more accurately, conservative Protestantism, went into hibernation as a culture-shaping force after the much publicized Scopes trial. The hibernation ended by the mid-1970s as the remnants of those forces who had advocated or at least assumed a common Protestant heritage in America could no longer countenance such obvious and major secular victories as ending prayer in school and the 1973 *Roe v. Wade* decision. Looking first (unsuccessfully) to Jimmy Carter in 1976 and then (much more successfully) to Ronald Reagan in 1980, the conservative Protestant controlled "Moral Majority," and now the "Christian Coalition," have become an effective—although certainly not societally dominant—political, cultural, and religious force in the United States.

How should orthodox Roman Catholics be expected to relate to contemporary conservative Protestantism? *Politically*, the relationship should be expected to be cordial and cooperative given a fundamental agreement on many specific and major issues (e.g., abortion, parental rights, pornography, religious representation in the public square, school vouchers, etc.). As Ralph Reed puts this, albeit a little too optimistically, "I believe that the emerging alliance, the emerging partnership of Catholics and Evangelical Protestants is going to be the most powerful force in the electorate in the 1990's and beyond."[1]

Culturally, the relationship should be ambivalent given an acknowledgment that there are both important similarities and differences between the conservative Protestant and orthodox Roman Catholic worldviews. Murray Friedman notes some important cultural congruencies: "Both had migrated from peasant backgrounds into the towns and cities of the country. Both had felt the stigma of being outsiders and resented deeply the 'cosmopolitan' culture. Their religious beliefs and social thought were based on common principles of family, neighborhood and roots."[2] Additionally and obviously, a belief that Christ is the Way, the Truth, and the Life will produce some common cultural threads; however, the varying methods by which this abstraction can be institutionalized into daily life will inevitably bring about cultural divergences. The typically conservative Protestant idolatry of early American society and of capitalism produces one set of serious historical and philosophical disagreements. The Catholic social principle of subsidiarity that is not necessarily antithetical to an important, albeit qualified, role for the federal government in American society is another potential area for serious disagreement.

Religiously, the relationship ought to be fraught with a certain amount of suspiciousness. Theologically, there are serious disagreements about many issues (e.g., the nature of the Church, authority, the human condition, the existence and applicability of the natural law, the created social order, etc.). This theological suspiciousness is only augmented further by considerable sociological evidence suggesting strong antipathy toward Roman Catholics on the part of contemporary conservative evangelical Protestants.[3]

In short, while open to a civil relationship, to political cooperation, and to a necessarily limited ecumenical exchange, Roman Catholics, if they are to be faithful to their own traditions and logic, must be basically prepared to "go it alone" making a distinctive Catholic contribution to the public square. As Rev. Neuhaus puts it so well:

> While we should judiciously cooperate with various alliances and coalitions, Catholics have a most particular responsibility. By virtue of our numbers, by virtue of the richness of our tradition, and by virtue of our worldwide communion with bishops in communion with the Bishop of Rome—who is Peter among us—ours is a distinctive responsibility and ours a singular role to play. If the Catholic Church is what she claims to be—and she is—she cannot be subsumed under any movement or cause or coalition or ideology, no matter how attractive. To those who would recruit the Church for the advancement of their agenda, whether they be of the left or of the right, we must lovingly but firmly say: The Bride of Christ is not for hire.[4]

While superior to the existing secular worldview, from a Roman Catholic perspective, evangelical Protestantism is but an incomplete splinter of the greater truth of Catholicism. Karl Adam puts it both bluntly and well:

Catholicism is according to its whole being the full and strong affirmation of the whole man, in the complete sum of all his life relations. Catholicism is the positive religion *par excellence*, essentially affirmation without subtraction, and in the full sense essentially thesis. All non-Catholic creeds are essentially anti-thesis, conflict, contradiction, and negation. And since negation is of its very nature sterile, therefore they cannot be creative, productive and original, or at least not in the measure in which Catholicism has displayed these qualities throughout the centuries. The modern man feels the positive character to be something that he needs, and therefore his gaze is turning towards Catholicism, if perchance it may do something for him.[5]

Like that of many other converts, recent and otherwise, the "positive character" of the Roman Catholic Church was something that the former Protestant evangelical, Thomas Howard, felt "he needed." As he stated at the time of his conversion:

I believe that the Roman Catholic Church is the Ancient Church. I accept its claims. I believe that here one finds the *fullness* ("catholicity") of the Faith. Hence, I mourn the splintering in Christendom. I pray daily for the reunion of Christ's Church.[6]

While declaring that "insofar as evangelicalism wants to open the Scriptures to all people and to love Jesus Christ the Lord, I am forever evangelical,"[7] Howard then moves on to suggest the insufficiency of evangelicalism regarding the worship of God in liturgy and sacrament. Among many other specific suggestions, he calls upon evangelicalism to return to legitimate episcopal authority, to the Eucharist as the focal point for Christian worship, and to the Liturgical year.[8] Similarly, Deal W. Hudson, a former Southern Baptist minister and now Catholic convert, argues that "all human beings...hunger for...[the] kind of liberation [that only Catholicism affords]."[9] For Hudson, the Catholic advantage was threefold:

First, it was totally liberating for a Baptist to realize that Christian intelligence is not limited merely to citing text from Scripture to support arguments, but rather that Christian intelligence takes in the whole of the natural order, and that God speaks through the natural order to the prudent eye....Second, it was liberating to realize that the biblical revelation, the revelation through the prophets, through Christ, had been contained, reflected and commented upon throughout the history of the Church, which is the body of Christ....[Finally] for a Baptist to come into the Catholic Mass, to realize that the culmination of worship does not come in response to a man's voice, however melodious, however articulate, but comes in response to the objective actual presence of Christ, was nothing less than a recovery of the full meaning of the Incarnation....These are the very issues—wisdom, doctrine, and worship—that give us our advantage in the public square.[10]

Evangelical Protestantism—or, for that matter, any other non-Catholic religion or philosophy—is simply not enough if America is ever to reach her fullest potential. Theologically, the Catholic Church is *the* Church of Christ. Sociologically, the Catholic Church is the only vehicle that satisfactorily expresses the total gamut of reality and human experience and adequately relates to each other the various dimensions of religiosity, that is, the *ritualistic, ideological, experiential, intellectualistic,* and *consequential,* as discussed by Glock and Stark.[11] But Catholicism cannot "do something" for America and her citizens if it is not faithfully presented in its total truth and beauty, according to its own logic and evolving tradition.

Notes

1.   Ralph Reed, Jr. "Catholic/Evangelical Relations," in *Public Catholicism: The Challenge of Living the Faith in a Secular Culture,* Thomas P. Melady, ed. (Huntington, Indiana: Our Sunday Visitor, 1996), 105.

2.   Murray Friedman, "Religion and Politics in an Age of Pluralism, 1945-1976: An Ethnocultural View," *Publius* 10, no. 3 (summer 1980): 69-70.

3.   Clyde Wilcox and Leopoldo Gomez, "The Christian Right and the Prolife Movement: An Analysis of the Sources of Political Support," *Review of Religious Research* 31, no. 4 (June 1990): 387.

4.   Rev. Richard J. Neuhaus, "Can Catholic Americans Be Trusted in the Public Square?" in *Public Catholicism: The Challenge of Living the Faith in a Secular Society,* Thomas P. Melady, ed. (Huntington, Indiana: Our Sunday Visitor, 1996), 47.

5.   Karl Adam, *The Spirit of Catholicism* (Garden City, New York: Image Books, 1954), 28.

6.   Thomas Howard, *Evangelical Is Not Enough: Worship of God in Liturgy and Sacrament,* 2nd ed. (San Francisco, California: Ignatius Press, 1988), 158.

7.   Howard, *Evangelical Is Not Enough,* 152.

8.   Howard, *Evangelical Is Not Enough,* 152-153.

9.   Deal Hudson, "What Cradle Catholics Take for Granted," in *Public Catholicism: The Challenge of Living the Faith in a Secular American Culture,* Thomas P. Melady, ed. (Huntington, Indiana: Our Sunday Visitor, 1996), 81.

10.   Hudson, "What Cradle Catholics Take for Granted," 80-81.

11.   Charles Glock and Rodney Stark, *Religion and Society in Tension* (Chicago, Illinois: Rand McNally, 1965).

Chapter Six

Reality Denied: On the Obsolescence of the Concept of the Natural Law

Paul E. Sigmund opens his volume, *Natural Law in Political Thought*, as follows:

> One of the prime targets of the current ferment in higher education is the irrelevance of much contemporary social science to fundamental moral problems. Current student concern is focused on the issues of authority, legitimacy, equality, war, sexuality, and community. These problems are not new to the history of moral and political theory. They have been discussed and analyzed before—and one of the principal methods used to resolve them, at least until the end of the eighteenth century, has been through the appeal to certain basic principles or values inherent in human nature—the theory of natural law.[1]

Natural law exists and has perennially existed. This philosophical position asserts that there is imposed into human organization a certain structure. Societal survival requires minimal conformity to this structure while flourishing societies require a fuller conformity. Furthermore, the natural law asserts that the human mind can grasp, at least roughly, through reason and its associated and subordinate faculties, the very nature of this structure. The idea of natural law historically has been accepted by most until the end of the eighteenth century by both atheist and believer and non-Christian and Christian alike. As Rev. John Courtney Murray so lucidly put it, "the life of man in society...is founded on truths, on a certain body of objective truth, universal in its import, accessible to the reason of man, definable, defensible." [2] The natural law, for Rev. Murray, makes the case "that man is intelligent; that reality is intelligible; and that reality, as grasped by intelligence, imposes on the will the obligation that it be obeyed in its demands for action or abstention."[3] Similarly, Paul E. Sigmund speaks of "a central assertion expressed or implied in most theories of natural law. This is the belief that there exists in nature and/or human nature a rational order which can provide intelligible value-statements independently of human will, that are universal in application, unchangeable in their ultimate content, and morally obligatory on mankind. These statements are expressed as laws or as moral imperatives which provide a basis for the evaluation of legal and political structures."[4]

With the appearance of the modern philosophies of Descartes and Kant started the descent into subjectivity, culminating in the rejection of the claim that there is an objective moral order that has certain inherent requirements. Speaking of the Cartesian and Kantian methods, Ralph McInerny notes that for both, "the world is measured by us, not the other way around. Man has become the measure. This is humanism gone mad."[5]

It is not, of course, that modernity has eliminated the reality of natural law; rather modernist modes of thought have denied this reality, making it much harder for the average individual to direct himself toward both understanding and conforming to the objective moral order. Following the famous sociological dictum of W. I. Thomas, "if something is defined as real, it is real in its consequences."[6] The natural law has been defined historically as unreal, as a specific and time-bound product of a by gone era, hence the obsolescence of the idea in the contemporary modern world.

The truth that the Catholic religion offers the world does not depend solely on its promulgation of the natural law. The Church relies also on Sacred Scripture and an ever developing Sacred Tradition for its understanding of reality. The natural law, however, represents the single greatest ecumenical tool that can bring a significant measure of peace, harmony, and justice to an imperfect world not under the influence of the Catholic faith. As Ralph McInerny puts it so well, given that "the main principles that should guide human conduct are naturally knowable by men...the theory...[of natural law] can be seen as the basis of exchange between believer and non-believer on moral matters. There is a common base they share."[7] Furthermore as discussed previously, the natural law is inevitably mediated through some religious-cultural matrix. Some religious-cultural formations, that is, those in the modern camp, retard the implementation of the natural law while others, that is, those in the classical camp, serve as effective carriers for it. The most effective mediator of the natural law is the total Catholic worldview. This is the case because the total Catholic worldview contains crucial elements other than the natural law—the Bible, Sacred Tradition, and Papal/Magisterial authority—which, methodologically, serve as a form of "triangularization" that keeps reason directed toward Truth. Thus, Catholicism's greatest contribution to the American public square is to serve as the mediator/carrier of the natural law.

This, in turn, requires a Catholic faith that is presented in a coherent manner. Unfortunately, Catholicism in post-Vatican II America lacks the required internal integrity and consistency to adequately represent the natural law in the American polity and civil society.

Notes

1. Paul E. Sigmund, *Natural Law in Political Thought* (Lanham, Maryland: University Press of America, 1971), v.
2. Rev. John Courtney Murray, *We Hold These Truths: Catholic Reflections on the American Proposition* (New York: Image Books, 1964), 8.
3. Rev. Murray, *We Hold These Truths*, 113.
4. Sigmund, *Natural Law*, viii.
5. Ralph McInerny, *A First Glance at St. Thomas: A Handbook for Peeping Thomists* (Notre Dame, Indiana: University of Notre Dame Press, 1990), 33.
6. W. I. Thomas and Dorothy S. Thomas, *The Child in America: Behavior Problems and Programs* (New York: Knopf, 1928), 572.
7. McInerny, *A First Glance*, 158.

Chapter Seven

Catholic Philosophical Vision, Catholic Historical Reality: The Need for a Catholic Plausibility Structure

The Catholic vision is a wondrously complex thing to contemplate in all its majesty. It is a vision even harder to institutionalize in the rounds of everyday existence.

It starts with a realistic anthropology. Human beings are primarily spiritual beings whose destiny, ideally and following St. Augustine, is to have one's soul rest with the Lord in Heaven. However, Catholicism, by no means, deprecates the material, the physical, the bodily. Our souls animate physical bodies that themselves are divine creations, reflections of a supernatural design that commands respect and inspires awe. As Karl Adam puts it so well, "Reverencing the body and defending human reason...[the Church] provides for the whole man." [1] Key here is the Catholic importance placed on a holistic understanding of man's reasoning potential which, in principle, is capable of both acknowledging and giving vent to but keeping necessarily subordinate his nonrational (e.g., emotional, erotic, intuitive) faculties. "The purpose of the Church," for Adam, is nothing less than..."the sanctification of men." [2]

The nature of the individual is portrayed as basically one oriented to do good but, as a result of original sin, with a concomitant tendency toward sin. Man is, likewise, capable of exercising a valid reason in the attempt to discover God, the truth, and the good life. While shaped by both supernatural and social influences, man is depicted as characterized by free will, which allows him to

51

choose his own course. Some, who choose to alienate themselves totally from God, will suffer the torments of hell.[3] Many others probably will temporarily find themselves in purgatory, a sphere of existence that so well exemplifies the Catholic understanding of God as one who dispenses simultaneously both justice and mercy.

In the Catholic worldview, the conscience is paramount only in those cases when it is properly formed by an authentic Catholic doctrinal sensibility and is consistent with the natural law. Given that man's reasoning ability is mitigated by his selfishness, less than omnipotent powers, and by the surrounding culture that may, in part or whole, be inconsistent with the faith, the grace of God and an active participation in the sacramental life that God has bestowed upon his Church to administer are, additionally, necessary to keep human beings more fully on course with their intended destiny. The faithful are also assisted in both reaching their supernatural destiny and fulfilling their religious-social obligations through an additional nexus to the divine, that is, through the communion of saints. The saints in Heaven intercede with Christ for success in the legitimate projects of the sinners of this world. Put another way, Catholics believe they go into daily battle (against their imperfect natures, against the selfishness of others, and against the principalities and powers) with hosts of invisible but real allies. The believing Catholic lives in a crowded, dense, and rich universe that spans both sides of the great divide.

The ideal Catholic individual blends, synthesizes, and combines many elements in his daily life: reason and faith, nature and grace, authority and conscience, action on behalf of justice and contemplative prayer, Church doctrine and personal devotion/private religious experience, intellect and mysticism, and universalism and particularism.[4] As Karl Adam points out, "It is quite true, Catholicism *is* a union of contraries. But contraries are not contradictories."[5] (The living saints, especially when surrounded by an inhospitable culture and hostile political forces, sometimes constitute the exception here, often personally concentrating and taking to its final logic, one or several of the aforementioned elements[6] but never at the price of questioning the broader Catholic worldview.) In the felicitous phrase of Karl Adam, Catholicism represents "an infinitely various yet unitary thing."[7] Furthermore, the Catholic faith, when transmitted properly, produces, for Adam, "a special Catholic temper, detachment from the world, yet no denial of natural values."[8]

The created order, likewise, has a structured purpose and inherent beauty and is, at base, good. Ideally, individuals, naturally in solidarity with other individuals, relate to each other in an interdependent, organic fashion. Put another way, the ordering principle of the Church—the Mystical Body of Christ—finds its contemporary social analogue, albeit a pale reflection, in a healthy functioning organic civilization. In other words, and following the Catholic concept of solidarity, individuals both naturally need and must take care of each other. This translates into a healthy Catholic respect for community and associational institutions, including political, governmental and international life. In the inspiring definition of John Paul II, given in *Sollicitudo Rei Socialis*,

#38, solidarity is defined as "a firm and persevering determination to commit oneself to the common good; that is to say to the good for all and of each individual, because we are *all* really responsible *for all*." [9] Furthermore, the concern for human solidarity extends across national borders as was made clear poignantly by Pope Paul VI in his *Populorum Progressio*.[10] Relatedly, the Catholic concept of the "universal purpose of goods," while affirming the need for private property, states that the goods of creation are meant for the benefit of all.

However, political and governmental life is intended to serve the ultimate and penultimate ends of human existence, that is, respectively, the salvation of souls and the creation of the good society. Regarding the former, in *Redemptoris Missio*, #5, John Paul II reaffirms the Church's mandate to evangelize, to preach the Gospel to all nations, to the whole world, to every creature.[11] Regarding the latter, the limiting of politics is found in the creation of a healthy civil society, which following the principle of "subsidiarity," consists of many groups and institutions, some primordial, some more consciously created, that stand between the individual and the megastructures of the public sphere. The most important of these intermediary institutions is the family, a "little Church" if you will, whose function is both procreation and the nurturing of good Christians and citizens.

The Catholic analogue to individualism, called personalism, stands between, on the one hand, various forms of collectivism, which subsume totally any independent status for the individual and, on the other, various forms of atomization in which the purpose and be-all of life center on the solitary individual. From the Catholic worldview, then, the individual has been born with certain constitutional rights and duties, although it is clear that society itself exists primarily to foster, first, the spiritual and, secondarily, the material needs of the individual.

Unlike the Protestant definition of the Church as purely an "invisible" reality, the Catholic Church, following especially the perspective of St. Robert Bellarmine, sees itself as a quite visible entity established directly by Christ. Furthermore, the Catholic self-understanding is that the Church is a divine institution characterized by an intimate and continual union with Christ. As Karl Adam declares, "Christianity…is a living stream of divine life flowing out from Christ and bearing His truth and His life, pure and uncontaminated, down the centuries."[12]

The Church, however, also has its human, imperfect face; as Karl Adam puts it, "the divine must necessarily suffer in its incarnation."[13] Adam continues, "as long as Catholicism lasts, it will feel the need for reform for a more perfect assimilation of its actuality to the ideal which illuminates its path.[14] Susceptible to occasional lapses in prudential judgment, the Church is nonetheless safeguarded "from above" from major errors of principle, given that she is directed by a Magisterial authority based on the reality of apostolic succession and protected by the Holy Spirit. This Magisterial authority, centered on the Pope as the Vicar of Christ, guarantees that the Church is the best and fullest interpreter of Sacred Scripture, Sacred Tradition, and the natural law.

The Catholic Church sees herself as the primary, albeit not exclusive, mediator between God and society and God and man. The Church never rejects what is true, holy, beautiful, and useful in the various cultures and subcultures of the world; the Church is an advocate of a realistic form of multiculturalism.[15] She understands both that there is salvation for those in good faith who are not visible members of the Church and that there is a reflection of divinity in all of God's creation; the task of the Church is to perfect human nature and society and bring them into the light of the Gospel. Although the divine deposit of revelation was fully completed by the end of the apostolic age, there is, following Cardinal John Henry Newman, a continual development of doctrine along organic lines as the absolute truth of Christ is itself mediated in different sociohistorical contexts.[16] One can properly speak, with appropriate qualifications, of an evolutionary movement of the Church over time in the direction of perfection as religious truth is seen as both cumulative and irreversible. Guided by the ability of the Magisterium to sift the chaff from the grain, the Catholic faith constantly accrues and adds valid historical interpretations of the faith to its evolving tradition, thus continually expanding the ability of mankind to understand better the will and design of God.

It is important to understand that it is *precisely* the wondrous and sophisticated nature of the Catholic vision that has made it the target of vicious secular and satanic attacks. *The Catholic faith is the only agency that is capable of providing an authentic alternative model to what today passes for what it means to be modern.* This is so because the Catholic faith does not, simply, reject science, high technology, the arts, the social sciences, the material world, the requirements of social justice for all, the body or the mind—all things of ultimate importance to the secular worldview and, in some sense, a prerequisite for participation in the modern world. Rather the Church both integrates and shapes these elements and concerns in an incredibly complex, albeit ultimately supernatural, vision that places them in a perspective proper to man's God-given nature and to God's design for mankind. Catholicism posits a "moderate dualism" between the supernatural and natural and the "other-worldly" and "this-worldly" that harmonizes the dyadic opposites previously referred to.

The Catholic vision of man, society, Church, and their interrelationship is simultaneously reasonable, balanced, subtle, and complex. It is, moreover, a highly fragile juxtapositioning of elements and relationships that requires a certain set of supportive institutional arrangements—called by sociologists a "plausibility structure"—to keep all the elements in their proper balance and relationship. Without an effective plausibility structure, what sociologically shapes individuals is not the "mind of the Church" but whatever is the prevalent religious-cultural message in a particular society in time and space.[17] Put crudely, given the finite and imperfect nature of individuals since the Fall, the Catholic Church as an ideal is too sophisticated for the average person to fully comprehend without an effective plausibility structure (or some special form of supernatural intervention).

The social science argument behind the concept of a plausibility structure is that *any* belief system requires a structural base that reaffirms, through constant social interaction and exposure, its "realness" to the individual. In somewhat technical language, Peter Berger states that:

> There is a further aspect...that is extremely important for the reality-maintaining task of religion. This aspect refers to the social-structural prerequisites of any religious...reality maintaining process. This may be formulated as follows: worlds are socially constructed and socially maintained. Their continuing reality, both objective (as common taken-for-granted facticity) and subjective (as facticity imposing itself on individual consciousness), depends on *specific* social processes, namely those processes that ongoingly reconstruct and maintain the particular worlds in question. Conversely, the interruption of these social processes threatens the (objective and subjective) reality of the worlds in question. Thus each world requires a social 'base' for its continuing existence as a world that is real to actual human beings. This 'base' may be called its plausibility structure.[18]

As James Hitchcock similarly puts it:

> Almost all knowledge is socially constructed, in the sense that very few individuals possess the security and courage to continue affirming ideas and apprehensions which society continuously denies, even if these apprehensions seem very real to the individual. The decline of religious faith, in a sense of the reality of God, is therefore a necessary result of the decline of the institutional Church. For the Church is a numerous, venerable, visible, and respected community of persons who publicly affirm, in a variety of ways, beliefs which in this culture are inherently improbable—God and the whole dimension of transcendence. As the institution shows itself vulnerable, as the individuals within it show themselves uncertain and groping, as many of its leaders abandon it, the beliefs and values which it has specifically affirmed become increasingly incredible. Those who are indifferent to the fate of the institution are, knowingly or unknowingly, also indifferent to the fate of religious belief, of historic Christianity.[19]

During the pre-Reformation period of Western Christendom in Europe, one can say that the larger society constituted a plausibility structure for Catholicism as most social institutions reinforced the presence of God and God's Church to the individual through his/her daily biographical existence. Historically, the Church found herself in a fundamentally different situation in the United States marked variously by either a Protestant or secular hegemony and/or a radical religious pluralism. In any event, the lack of a common Catholic culture in the United States necessitates that the Church continually builds and maintains a plausibility structure. The Catholic plausibility structure started to take shape after World War I and hit full stride in the 1940s and 1950s only to be severely weakened by both external and internal forces in the post-Vatican II period.

Historically, in the United States, the plausibility structure of the Catholic Church has been weakest both in its earliest and contemporary periods. Only during the period from World War I through the 1960s—the institutional fruits of the Baltimore Councils and Plenary Sessions held from 1829 to 1884—could it be said that the Church's philosophical vision was effectively, albeit still imperfectly, transmitted to the Catholic population. As Philip Gleason so astutely has observed, "for the Catholics of the 1930s, it was the capacity of their vision to integrate, to unify all spheres of life, that made it so appealing and convinced them it offered a remedy for the social atomization and spiritual emptiness of a civilization torn by clashing ideologies and unchecked social and economic forces."[20] The sociological presupposition for the effective evangelization of the Catholic worldview for both the Catholic population at large and into the American public square lies in the rebuilding of a Catholic plausibility structure.

The evidence that an internally cohesive and consistent Catholic plausibility structure is necessary for the evangelization and maintenance of the faith in the United States is overwhelming.[21] The early colonial period of Catholic history in this country, characterized by its absence of theological and social organizational unity and by an insufficient number of clergy, parishes, personnel and financial supports, saw massive defections to either Protestant Christianity or to the lapsed condition of the unchurched. The early answer to Bishop Gerald Shaughnessy's classic question, "Has the immigrant kept the faith?" was often a simple "No." Ironically, this is the very historical stage, that is, the "Republican interlude" that is aggrandized by such progressive scholars as Jay Dolan[22] as an early "age of the laity" that was prophetic of things to come after Vatican II. In a perverse way, Dolan is correct.

The outlines for an effective Catholic plausibility structure in the United States were devised in the seven provincial sessions and in the three national plenary councils of Baltimore that started in 1829 and lasted until 1884. The blueprint for the invidiously referred to "Catholic ghetto" took on life as doctrine was standardized; renegade clergy were disciplined; and churches, schools, hospitals and other infrastructure requirements were built. Bishop Gerald Shaughnessy could legitimately quip that the bishops "built the Church in the United States better than they knew."[23] This structure grew and strengthened itself, jelling after World War I. Speaking of the year 1957, the orthodox Jewish scholar, Will Herberg, observed that "the Catholic Church in America operates a vast network of institutions of almost every type and variety....This immense system constitutes at one and the same time a self-contained Catholic world with its own complex interior economy and American Catholicism's resources for participation in the larger American community." [24] As Monsignor George A. Kelly puts it, "as a *tour de force* by a religious group, the institutional and community accomplishments of the American Church are unsurpassed in Catholic history. Though the tendency today is to accentuate the deficiencies of the American Church, there are those who think that its equal cannot be found anywhere."[25] What were some of the positive benefits of the post-World War II, pre-Vatican II Catholic plausibility structure that is today so battered and under relentless attack from Catholic progressives? Monsignor Kelly lists five:

> 1) The overwhelming majority of the Catholic people had been effectively reached by the Church's manifold structures. They were practicing Catholics.
> 2) The Church through its supported family life and school systems became the instrument of Americanization and upward social mobility.
> 3) The leaders of the Church—Bishops, priests, religious, lay apostles—won the loyalty of the vast numbers of Catholics in major matters involving Church doctrine and Church policy.
> 4) Catholic parishes for the most part were important local communities. Sometimes they were solely ethnic, most often neighborhood centers for Catholics, and occasionally social communities that related successfully to indigenous non-Catholics and to custodians of municipal affairs.
> 5) The institutional Church also presided over the emergence of a Catholic elite—mainly through its colleges, seminaries, and lay apostolic movements for social justice, international peace, family life, and spiritual perfection. These movements owed their existence to the impetus given them by the Holy See from Leo XIII onward. Even the loyal opposition (typified by John Courtney Murray and Dorothy Day) proposed new approaches and new accommodations within the framework of the Church structure.[26]

Accepting the argument of Monsignor Kelly, one can state that between the years 1917 and the opening of the Vatican II era in the United States, the Catholic Church was a vital and distinctive subcultural reality, that is, that its plausibility structure was functioning well. One can say this without endorsing every characteristic of this period and without arguing that there was no room for improvement or development.

But why has the post-Vatican II Catholic plausibility structure now been so weakened? The increasingly dominant Americanizer and heterodox wing of the Church argues that the destruction of what it invidiously referred to as the Catholic "ghetto" was both necessary and inevitable. It was inevitable given the claim that such a deinstitutionalization would have happened with or without the occurrence of Vatican II. Vatican II is viewed here as the Church's belated response to the themes of modernity. That Vatican II occurred when it did only speeded up an inevitable Americanization/modernization process. Simultaneously speaking out of both sides of their mouths, Americanizers also argue that the destruction of the "ghetto" was called for by at least the spirit of Vatican II, the ghetto allegedly creating a Catholic mentality and stance to the world at odds with the necessary modern, progressive, ecumenical worldview. Orthodox

Roman Catholics see it otherwise. The Catholic plausibility structure existing before the 1960s could have and should have been updated in light of a *literal* understanding of Vatican II and not, for practical purposes, destroyed. The damage done to the Catholic subculture was neither sociologically inevitable nor theologically called for by Vatican II. Indeed, a correct understanding of Vatican II requires a cohesive and distinctive Catholic plausibility structure in order to fulfill the Catholic task of "Christianizing the temporal sphere" in America and elsewhere.

Notes

1.   Karl Adam, *The Spirit of Catholicism* (Garden City, New York: Image Books, 1954), 13.
2.   Adam, *Spirit*, 13.
3.   St. Robert Bellarmine, *Hell and Its Torments* (Rockford, Illinois: Tan Books, 1990).
4.   Joseph A. Varacalli, "Multiculturalism, Catholicism, and American Civilization," *Homiletic and Pastoral Review* 94, no. 6 (March 1994): 47-55. Joseph A. Varacalli, "Whose Justice and Justice for What Purpose?: A Catholic Neo-Orthodox Critique," *International Journal of Politics, Culture, and Society* 6, no. 2 (winter 1992): 309-321.
5.   Adam, *Spirit*, 20.
6.   Pitirim A. Sorokin, *Altruistic Love: A Study of American Good Neighbors and Christian Saints* (Boston, Massachusetts: Beacon Press, 1950).
7.   Adam, *Spirit*, 9.
8.   Adam, *Spirit*, 14.
9.   Pope John Paul II, *Sollicitudo Rei Socialis, #38*, in *Aspiring to Freedom: Commentaries on John Paul II's Encyclical 'The Social Concerns of the Church,'* Kenneth A. Myers, ed. (Grand Rapids, Michigan: Eerdmans, 1988).
10.   Pope Paul VI, *Populorum Progressio*, 1967.
11.   Pope John Paul II, *Redemptoris Missio*, 1990.
12.   Adam, *Spirit*, 10.
13.   Adam, *Spirit*, 14.
14.   Adam, *Spirit*, 230.
15.   Varacalli, "Multiculturalism," 51-52, 54. Joseph A. Varacalli, "The Saints in the Lives of Italian-American Catholics: Toward a Realistic Multiculturalism," in *The Saints in the Lives of Italian-Americans: An Interdisciplinary Investigation*, Joseph A. Varacalli et al., eds. (Stony Brook, New York: Forum Italicum, 1999), 231-249.
16.   John Henry Cardinal Newman, *Essay on the Development of Christian Doctrine* (New York, 1845).
17.   Joseph A. Varacalli, "'Homophobia' at Seton Hall University: Sociology in Defense of the Faith," *Faith and Reason* 20, no. 3 (fall 1994): 303.
18.   Peter L. Berger, *The Sacred Canopy: Elements of a Sociological Theory of Religion* (New York: Doubleday, 1967), 45.
19.   James Hitchcock, *The Decline and Fall of Radical Catholicism* (New York: Image Books, 1972), 109.
20.   Philip Gleason, *Keeping the Faith: American Catholicism Past and Present* (Notre Dame, Indiana: University of Notre Dame Press, 1987), 29.

21.   Joseph A. Varacalli, "A Catholic Plausibility Structure," *Homiletic and Pastoral Review* 89, no. 2 (November 1988): 66-67.

22.   Jay P. Dolan, *The American Catholic Experience* (New York: Doubleday, 1985). Jay P. Dolan, "Letter to the Editor: Reply to Varacalli," *The American Historical Review* 91, no. 5 (December 1986): 1322. Joseph A. Varacalli, "Book Review, Jay P. Dolan's *The American Catholic Experience*," *The American Historical Review* 91, no. 3 (June 1986): 726-727. Joseph A. Varacalli, "Reply to Jay P. Dolan," *The American Historical Review* 91, no. 5 (December 1986): 1322-1323.

23.   Bishop Gerald Shaughnessy quoted in Monsignor George A. Kelly, *The Battle for the American Church Revisited* (San Francisco, California: Ignatius Press, 1995), 39.

24.   Will Herberg, *Protestant, Catholic, Jew: An Essay in Religious Sociology* (New York: Anchor Books, 1960), 153-154.

25.   Monsignor George A. Kelly, *The Battle for the American Church* (New York: Doubleday, 1979), 456.

26.   Monsignor Kelly, *The Battle*, 456.

Chapter Eight

Post-World War II American Catholicism: Anticipating the Catholic Moment

There is an interesting debate within the circles of orthodox Catholicism that centers on the significance and state of the Catholic Church in the immediate post-World War II scene in the United States. All orthodox Catholics agree that this period of time represents the historical height of Catholic influence and institutional integrity; the debate centers on whether or not it represented a realized "Catholic moment" in American history.

Viewed in terms of many external indicators, a strong argument can be made that the Church had, during that era, a special moment. The Church was growing in size, her population was ever more formally educated, ever more middle-class, ever more orthodox in belief and practice. Religious orders, seminaries and parishes were filled to the brim with priests, sisters, and brothers. Mass attendance was perhaps the highest in the recorded history of the Church universal. The number of Catholic schools—from the grammar through higher educational levels—was on the increase. Catholics were a respected, albeit secondary, part of the F.D.R. coalition and, paraphrasing Glazer and Moynihan, Fordham University graduates were replacing Harvard University graduates in important government jobs.[1] The Church was admired in popular films and feared by defenders of a Protestant hegemony, like Paul Blanshard.[2] Orthodox, conservative Catholic authors were published by secular presses and their books were published in the hundreds of thousands. Bishop Fulton J. Sheen's homilies and speeches were received enthusiastically by many non-Catholics; conversions to the faith were high. No less respected a Catholic intellectual than

Monsignor George A. Kelly would term this period in time and space as one of "gold status" for the Church, viewed from the frame of reference of not only America but that of the Church Universal.[3] Up until recently, I both accepted and developed Monsignor Kelly's perspective in my own writings.[4]

I have changed my mind at least in degree.[5] One reason for the change is my recognition of the inability of those defending this position to answer satisfactorily the question as to why Catholicism—if so internally strong up to the mid-1960s—so quickly folded in the immediate wake of the Council and the social upheavals of the time. Another reason lies in the distinction between the institutional integrity of Catholic America and the ability of those institutions to transform America; simply put, up until 1965, an admittedly cohesive Catholic America was not as successful as many Catholics would have hoped in shaping the direction of American public life. There were not many convincing signs, for instance, of Catholic social doctrine competing successfully in the public square against either quasi-capitalist or quasi-socialist formulations. Even President Franklin D. Roosevelt's "New Deal" (which, admittedly, was somewhat influenced by the Bishops' Program of Social Reconstruction published in 1919 and penned by Monsignor John A. Ryan) and the American union movement (which, admittedly, was not inconsequentially shaped by Catholic thinkers and workers) developed in ways significantly at variance with Catholic social thought.

Perhaps any Catholic transformation of America would require first the widespread rejection of the established liberal, individualist order for the faith to successfully, in a sociological sense, "move in." And mainstream Protestantism, at least in the 1960s, was still filling successfully, in a sociological sense, what is now recognized as a societal moral vacuum. Perhaps the then tribal nature of the Catholic community—fragmented into different religious orders and ethnic bases—hindered such a transformation. Perhaps the Americanist/modernist/ assimilationist impulse in American Catholicism, seemingly defeated at the turn of the twentieth century, was still a viable and potent undercurrent in American Catholic life just waiting for an historical opening to reemerge with a vengeance. Perhaps the reigning Catholic orthodoxy in the post-World War II scene was too superficial, too unchallenged, too uncritical, and too eroded by a complacent acceptance of an easy and uncomplicated assimilation into the American Dream.[6] Conversely put, perhaps a Catholic moment in America presupposes going through, and responding creatively to, a this-worldly period of oppression. Or perhaps any true Catholic moment, as Catholic neoconservatives are wont to contend, required the ideas and vision of Vatican II.

Whether Vatican II was or was not a presupposition for the emergence of an authentic Catholic moment can and will be debated. Perhaps the Catholic moment in America could have evolved minus the interactive and exponential impact of the Second Vatican Council with the cultural revolutions of the mid-1960s through the 1980s. Perhaps a Catholic moment would have been ensured if Vatican II had been convened shortly after World War II. What seems to be clear to this author, in retrospect, is that a 1950s Catholicism in the United States can best be seen as *anticipating* an authentically Catholic moment, a moment further away at this writing than it was during the 1950s due, primarily, to unnecessary self-inflicted wounds in the Catholic body and despite the grand vision of Vatican II and the writings and stature of John Paul II.

Notes

1.   Nathan Glazer and Patrick J. Moynihan, *Beyond the Melting Pot: The Negroes, Puerto Ricans, Jews, Italians, and Irish of New York City* (Cambridge, Massachusetts: M.I.T. Press, 1970).

2.   Paul Blanshard, *American Freedom and Catholic Power* (Boston, Massachusetts: Beacon Press, 1949).

3.   Monsignor George A. Kelly, *Inside My Father's House* (New York: Doubleday, 1989), 16.

4.   See, especially Joseph A. Varacalli, "'Those Were the Days': Church and American Society in the 1940s and 1950s," *Faith and Reason* 16, no. 1 (spring 1990): 81-89.

5.   See especially, Joseph A. Varacalli, "Catholic Conservatism—Does It Exist? Where Is It Going?" *Lay Witness* 16, no. 10 (November/December 1995): 12-13, 30.

6.   See the discussion of the superficial religious commitments of the era by Will Herberg, *Protestant, Catholic, Jew: An Essay in Religious Sociology* (New York: Anchor Books, 1960). Also see Gordon Allport's discussion of "immature religion" in his *The Individual and His Religion* (New York: Macmillan, 1960).

Chapter Nine

Secularization from Within: The Post-Vatican II Catholic Church in America

In his justly celebrated analysis of modern religion, Peter L. Berger made the distinction between two processes both weakening the impact of traditional religion on the institutions of society and on individual human consciousness. The first process, more obvious, overt and typical of Western Europe, he termed "secularization from without." In this form, secularism simply fills the void, either socially or individually, vacated by traditional symbols and modes of thought. The second process, typical in the United States—while no less corrosive to authentic religion—is much more subtle and subdued. Berger referred to the latter as "secularization from within." In this form, traditional religion remains, albeit as a hollowed out, ineffective reality, little more than providing a thin veneer for what is actually and effectively nonreligious belief and practice.[1]

What has occurred within Catholicism in the post-Vatican II era in American society is precisely an example of a pervasive "secularization from within." The vision of Vatican II—which actually and objectively stands in both an organic and developmental relationship with two thousand years of prior Catholic tradition—has failed to be implemented in the American context. Rather what has been ushered in has been a notoriously selective understanding of the conciliar and post-conciliar documents along decidedly progressive lines. Put another way, the deformed spirit and not the substance and law of Vatican II has been interpreted in such a way by the presently dominant "Americanist" leadership as to make it practically identical with a highly secularized version of either a generic liberal Protestantism or a slightly more inclusive American Civil Religion.[2]

The successful carriers of this bogus vision of the faith is an elite "new Catholic knowledge class"[3] composed of intellectuals, bureaucrats, social activists, and social policy planners whose legitimacy is based on secular educational credentials and who stand in a fundamental class conflict with those bishops loyal to Catholic tradition whose authority resides "from up high" based as it is on the concept of apostolic succession. The emergence of the new Catholic knowledge class to a dominant status in the post-conciliar Church represents a startling victory for the modernist and assimilationist wing beaten back at the turn of the century and marks a sudden reversal in the operant frame of reference for "Catholic" intellectuals, from that of a Magisterially defined tradition to that of an essentially secular worldview. The inspiration of the new Catholic knowledge class is not only clearly from non-Catholic sources but is, furthermore, buttressed by a quite worldly set of status, power, and economic interests.

Theological Distortions

Examples of how a "secularization from within" operates today within the Church are abundant. In terms of a general theological worldview, certain statements are taken out of their proper context within the documents of Vatican II and post-Vatican II official theology and used to transform radically what passes for the Faith. The Church "as the People of God" is used to promote a false and disingenuous democratic attitude. It is false because the Council did *not* (and *could* not) abandon the age-old argument that final authority rests with the Magisterium. It is disingenuous because its effect is anything but democratic, substituting the authority of one set of elites, the new Catholic knowledge class, for another, that is, the Pope and those bishops in loyal communion with him. "The People of God" metaphor is actually sociologically employed as a lifeless abstraction like that of the "victims of injustice" whose "cause" the new class utilizes in its grab for increased status, power, and employment within the large Church bureaucracy. The importance of a properly formed Christian conscience degenerates in progressivist thought into an autonomous individualism. The concern for the institutionalization of social justice is, in a knee-jerk fashion, translated into promoting utopian and failed socialist thought and into supplanting in importance the ultimate goal of the Catholic faith, that is, the salvation of souls. A legitimate concern for ecumenical relations based on discovering those "rays of truth" found in other religions and in the cross-cultural commonalities of natural law thinking and practice is transfigured into the common liberal arguments for moral relativism and that all major religions are equal in their truth content, reflecting but different aspects of one greater truth. Speaking of liberal religion in its popular mode, Julia Mitchell Corbett puts it well: "liberal religion emphasizes the equality of all religions…the comparative study of religion is important because it provides a variety of perspectives that can enrich and complement each other. Truth is one, but it has many faces."[4] That the Catholic faith itself has legitimately harnessed pluralism in the pursuit of truth is a reality apparently lost in the consciousness of progressive Catholics and secularists alike.

A National Bureaucracy with a Mind of Its Own

Examples of a secularization from within can be concretized somewhat by analyzing the official statements of the national bureaucracy, that of the N.C.C.B./U.S.C.C. The analysis of J. Brian Benestad, for instance, in reviewing the policy statements of the U.S. Catholic Bishops from 1966 through to 1980, is particularly revealing. His general thesis is that, at the national level, the bishops, in issuing a myriad number of specific social policy statements—many of them on trendy liberal issues—have neglected their two primary duties in the social sphere, that is, evangelization and the teaching of Catholic social doctrine. More specifically, Benestad contends that the bishops have (1) issued statements in which they lack sufficient expertise; (2) failed to communicate satisfactorily the Church's rich social doctrine; (3) failed to instruct and involve the laity in their task of Christianizing the temporal sphere; (4) demonstrated a politically partisan attitude by focusing mainly on issues of importance to political progressives; (5) neglected, for the most part, the principle of subsidiarity and, conversely, overplayed the role of the federal government in the pursuit of the good society; and (6) have relinquished their responsibility for the forging of social policy to an unrepresentative and left-wing group of new class bureaucrats centered in and around the United States Catholic Conference.[5]

Analyses published subsequently to Benestad's variously develop and apply his critique and provide further evidence of an encroaching "secularization from within." George Weigel argued that the 1983 publication of the much celebrated N.C.C.B./U.S.C.C. pastoral, *The Challenge of Peace*, marked the decisive abandonment of the "hardheaded idealism" or "moderate realism" by which the Catholic tradition hitherto approached the political order.[6] This tradition—which had tread a middle road between Hobbesian and utopian thought—has now been, for Weigel, skewed in the direction of the latter in the form of a softer, psychologically oriented, semi-pacificist line of thought that is a blend of a selective interpretation of biblical ideas with secular currents, the latter including an acceptance of a quasi-Marxist understanding of the role that the United States plays in world affairs.

Monsignor George A. Kelly takes a related but somewhat different track in his critique of *The Challenge of Peace*; it is a critique, nonetheless, that offers evidence of another example of an internal secularization. For Monsignor Kelly, the first two drafts contained "consequentialist" thinking that, if not eliminated, could be abstracted from the pastoral and applied to all forms of Catholic doctrine. As he stated, "in other words, if one can do evil to gain some good, then pragmatism, not principle and doctrine, governs life, including Catholic life, no matter what Christ and the Church has to say about it."[7] The key erroneous sentence, for Monsignor Kelly, reads as follows: "The *deterrence relationship* which prevails between the United States, the Soviet Union, and other powers is *objectively a sinful situation* because of the threats implied in it and the consequences it has in the world."[8] As he comments, "the original drafts were willing to tolerate the evil situation because failure of deterrence would be worse."[9] Through the intervention of Cardinal Ratzinger and then Bishop John O'Connor, the final draft had accepted the judgment issued by Pope John Paul II at the United Nations in June of 1982 to the effect that deterrence is not, in and by itself, sinful. As His Holiness stated at the time, "In current conditions [deterrence] based on balance, certainly not an end in itself but as a step on the way toward a progressive disarmament may still be judged morally acceptable."[10] Only after such intervention was the sentence promoting consequentialism purged in the final draft published on May 3, 1983.

Following closely on the heels of the nuclear weapons statement was the next major and controversial N.C.C.B./U.S.C.C. pastoral on the American economy, *Economic Justice for All*, published on November 13, 1986. The politically correct nature of this document lies mainly in the section proposing social policies that could easily have come from out of the left wing of the Democratic Party. And while the bishops make clear that their judgments and recommendations concerning social policy do not carry the same authority as do their statements regarding universal moral principles and formal Church teachings, the simple fact remains that they *did* advocate highly partisan viewpoints. As James K. Fitzpatrick tellingly inquires, "to be sure, one might ask why, after making this admission, the bishops nonetheless felt obliged to delve into these specific issues."[11] Father Avery Dulles applies Fitzpatrick's critique of the economic pastoral to much of the post-1960s statements of the American bishops when he observes that

> the bishops claim to be speaking as pastors, not as experts on military affairs, economics, or whatever. But when they make detailed applications of the kind I have mentioned, this distinction is hard to maintain. Recognizing the importance of secular input, the bishops conduct hearings to learn the views of experts and rely on specialists to draft their documents. Thus they implicitly acknowledge the inseparability of their conclusions from the facts and theories they accept from their consultants. They make choices among views that are held by sincere and intelligent Catholics....Because the specific applications cannot be vindicated from Scripture or tradition, I think that it is generally wise for the bishops to avoid lending their authority to one position or the other. When they intervene in controversial questions of a secular character they stir up opposition to themselves from within the Church and therefore undermine their own authority to teach and govern.[12]

As Monsignor George A. Kelly relatedly states, "the economic pastoral is a good example of the ideological bias of staff writers and chosen consultants. Since so much of the popes' social criticism has been anticapitalistic, Catholics cannot be blind to the evils of the American system. But Catholic writers, in spite of the insistence of the same popes on the rights of property owners, can be overly statist."[13] Indeed, Monsignor Kelly provides evidence of the statist inclinations of the staff writers of the pastoral by noting that the first two drafts underplayed the importance of a cohesive family life and of Catholic education in furthering the integral development of the poor. As he states, "these omissions in the earlier drafts surprised some bishops in view of the long tradition of emphasizing family and school in evangelization. Good family life was the important insulating force against the worst features of poverty. Often poor but well-integrated families did not know they were poor. Catholic schools, moreover, were the chief instruments for Americanizing the children of earlier immigrants. So it was important for the economic pastoral to recall this heritage, even if belatedly."[14]

Monsignor Kelly's critique, however, goes beyond the charge of statism and includes specific instances of neglecting Catholic doctrine, at least in the early drafts of *Economic Justice for All*. Malthusian-like terminology regarding "exponential" population growth and phrases like "quality of life" and "responsible parenthood," which were originally included, were, in the final draft, either dropped—as in the first two cases—or surrounded with Catholic qualifiers—as in the last case with the addition of a long quote by Paul VI on population policy. As Monsignor Kelly so astutely [and sadly] observed, "something is wrong when bishops' pastorals are composed in the public forum incorrectly, leaving the responsible authors [hierarchy] needlessly embarrassed at having 'outsiders' [and this would include Rome] correct a U.S. Catholic document, when in a normal situation an official draft of a Church viewpoint should have been well-nigh perfect."[15]

In his important chapter five, "American Bishops and the Catholic Issues," of his volume *Keeping the Church Catholic with John Paul II*, Monsignor Kelly then proceeds to document the pervasive "secularization from within" that is evidenced through other important statements of the N.C.C.B./U.S.C.C. published throughout the 1980s. Among others, there were statements that (1) suggested the propriety of educational efforts that "include accurate information about prophylactic devices or other practices proposed by some medical experts as potential means of preventing AIDS,"[16] (2) called for "further study" on the issue of the ordination of women[17] and (3) unduly juridicized and tended to level the authority relationship between bishops and theologians.[18]

Another more recent analysis confirms the previous line of thought. Michael Warner has aptly referred to the "changing witness" on public policy of the American Bishops through the N.C.C.B./U.S.C.C. bureaucracy. For Warner:

The bishops' reorganization of the N.C.W.C into the N.C.C.B. and U.S.C.C. brought in new personnel, processes, and ideas....In the late 1960s, the reformed and expanded U.S.C.C. secretariat took in new advisors who reoriented the message of the bishops' conference. Inspired by European notions of a "political theology," the U.S.C.C. staff prompted the bishops to take critical stands on newly designated "moral issues," particularly poverty and the Vietnam War. The new political theology was not a true reading of Vatican II, however....The old N.C.W.C. had promoted Catholic social doctrine as the fulfillment of reason—as the full and true exposition of the natural law that was attainable only in the light of Christ. The N.C.C.B., however...has regarded the Church's God-given wisdom more as a "resource" than an imperative....Conference statements after the 1960s only rarely tried to show how the truth revealed by Jesus Christ benefits all society; instead they emulated the policy pronouncements of secular lobbies and interest groups by criticizing current policies, advocating new ones, and calling generally for cooperation, planning, and peace.[19]

Michael Warner concludes his analysis by comparing the authentic Catholic stance of John Paul II with the body of American bishops. As he states:

But the social magisterium of John Paul II provides an alternative model: one that transcends the sterile options of cultural accommodation or "pragmatic" compromise with modern ideological error. By focusing the social doctrine of the Church on the moral and cultural foundations of democracy and the free economy, the Pope has diagnosed the pathologies that affect American liberty, and threaten its capacity to promote justice for all.[20]

The Destruction of the Catholic Plausibility Structure

Perhaps a useful way to start our analysis of the internal secularization within other institutions of Catholic life is to recall the thesis so confidently predicted in 1976 by Rev. Andrew Greeley in his volume, *The Communal Catholic*. For Greeley:

In the next ten years Catholicism, *as an ecclesiatical institution in the United States*, will continue in the course of its precipitous decline. At the same time, however, American Catholics, *as a community in our society*...will experience a dramatic increase in healthy self-consciousness and self-awareness. By "ecclesiastical institution" I mean the organized church: the hierarchy, the priesthood, the religious orders of women and men, and the various institutions which are administered by those groups of people—schools, orphanages, hospitals, charitable institutions, organizations of laity directly under church control, as well as newspapers, magazines, and other forms of communication with an official or quasi-official character. I also include those subsidiary institutions that...exist mostly to service it—religious goods stores, newspapers, and magazines whose primary focus is the institutional church. By the "Catholic community"...I mean Catholics as a collectivity within the larger

American population. The Catholic community in the sense that I use it here is roughly equivalent to the "Jewish community" or the "black community." It refers to a populace rather than to an organized structure.[21]

More than twenty years after Rev. Greeley's pontification, it is transparently clear that his thesis is only half-right: *both* post-Vatican II "ecclesiastical institution" and "Catholic community" are continuing on with their "precipitous decline." Furthermore, the unthinking assimilation of many American Catholics into the tenets of secularism and liberal Protestantism is due *precisely* to the self-afflicted destruction or at least weakening of what Rev. Greeley refers to as the "ecclesiastical institution." Again, the network of ecclesiastical and ecclesiastically affiliated institutions referred to invidiously as the "Catholic ghetto" is a sociologically necessary, although not a theologically sufficient, condition for an authentic Catholicism to thrive.

One can point to many examples of the religious and moral rot found within the once solidly Catholic nature of the Church's ecclesiatical institutions. Many priests in their parishes today, purposely or unselfconsciously, blur the important distinction between God's infinite mercy with the uncritical acceptance of a therapeutic mentality.[22] Psychologist William Kirk Kilpatrick, for instance, speaks of a priest in one Catholic Church who tells his congregation, "The purpose of Christ's coming was to say, 'You're O.K. and I'm O.K.'" Kilpatrick continues, "In other churches, parents are told that their children are incapable of sinning, because 'that's what psychologists tell us.'...Almost everywhere, salvation is being equated with self-growth or feelings of O.K.-ness. In short, Christians have let their faith become tangled in a net of popular ideas about self-esteem and self-fulfillment that aren't Christian at all."[23] As such, sociologist James O'Kane's (1991) study indicating that priests are themselves going to confession less often today than in previous decades should come as no surprise.[24]

Another important example of "secularization from within" can be provided through reference to the direction taken by Catholic religious education, or what Monsignor Michael Wrenn has termed the "catechetical establishment," in the United States since the Council. As Monsignor Wrenn has put it:

Previously the Church and her beliefs and practices had been scorned and attacked primarily by bigots from outside the Church; suddenly all these things came under attack by the newly sophisticated within the Church who compared the Church with the world outside and too often found her sadly wanting. Pope John XXIII's calling of a council to "update" the Church was exactly what these Catholics had been waiting for; they knew exactly in what respects the Church needed to be updated, and it usually turned out to be almost anything that was "traditional."[25]

This progressive catechetical establishment is, of course, yet another wing of the "new Catholic knowledge class." Predictably, its present major focus is to blunt an orthodox implementation in the United States of the very instrument that orthodox defenders of the faith expect to be vital in any authentic restoration, that is, the *Catechism of the Catholic Church.*

Relatedly, many of the older, established, and once distinguished religious orders of the Church are now emaciated and riddled with dissent. Speaking of the post-Vatican II transformation of the Society of Jesus in the United States, James Hitchcock bluntly states that "an 'openness' to newer modes of thought soon became, for many, a wholesale acceptance of systems which could be reconciled with Catholicism only with difficulty if at all, and a concomitant compulsion to brush aside almost everything from the Catholic past as irrelevant at best, perhaps even false and pernicious. The most contested areas have been almost all aspects of sexual morality, from contraception to homosexuality, as well as the general exercise of ecclesiastical authority by pope and bishops."[26] Psychologist William Coulson makes similar observations about the devastation he has witnessed over the past few decades regarding not only the Jesuits but also within the Sisters of Mercy, the Sisters of Providence and especially within the Sisters of the Immaculate Heart of Mary.[27]

To address another example of the present day failure of Catholic institutions to perform their duties properly, more than a few Catholic mass media outlets have turned into showcases for dissident thought and activity. Catholic priest and author Gerard Morrissey makes the point by quoting an April 1981 letter from the then-Apostolic delegate of the Holy See to the United States, Archbishop Pio Laghi, to the American bishops:

> With increasing frequency the Holy See receives letters from the United States complaining about articles appearing in Catholic newspapers, including diocesan publications, which cause harm to the Faith of the people because of a lack of respect for the teaching and decisions of the Magisterium. As you know, it is not unusual for such articles to contain criticisms and attacks even on the teaching authority and the person of the Holy Father. The impact of such criticism is heightened when columns are syndicated and widely circulated....[What is needed is] the promotion of a sound and vital Catholic press, so useful an instrument for evangelization and so vibrant in the life of the Church in the United States.[28]

Catholic educational institutions now routinely harbor and promote many ideas other than those Catholic.[29] As Philip Gleason has pointed out, in the post-Vatican II era, "the old ideological structure of Catholic education...[that is, neo-scholasticism]...had been swept away entirely."[30] For Gleason, "the task facing Catholic academics today is to forge from the philosophical and theological resources uncovered in the past half-century a vision that will provide what Neoscholasticism did for so many years—a theoretical rationale for the existence of Catholic colleges and universities as a distinctive element in American higher education." [31] Monsignor George A. Kelly puts it more bluntly than does Gleason and assigns more self-conscious responsibility to the actors involved for the present-day debacle of Catholic higher education: "the heroes of the post-Vatican II Church, at least if one follows journalistic opinion or studies the favorite authors of well-touted magazines or scans the standard list of consultants of the National Conference of Catholic Bishops, invariably are university administrators or faculty who are intimately tied into public dissent from the magisterium."[32] Furthermore, the progressive establishment has been shockingly successful in blunting the impact of Rome's vision for Catholic higher education, *Ex corde Ecclesiae*, and had been able to get N.C.C.B./U.S.C.C. approval, in November 1996, for an incredibly weak set of Ordinances allegedly intended to implement the Apostolic Constitution.[33] While not officially sanctioned, some Catholic seminaries nonetheless either attract or cast a wayward eye toward active homosexual activity. Even more egregiously, Paul Likoudis reports that at a March 1997 conference sponsored by New Ways Ministry, two Catholic bishops openly promoted the homosexual agenda in Catholic institutions.[34] And as Rev. Enrique Rueda and Michael Schwartz caution, "it is crucial to understand how extensively the homosexual movement has already infiltrated our country's mainline churches....Churches, once they have been infiltrated by the homosexual movement, constitute one of its most important allies. Not only because of the ideological and human support they provide, but also on account of the availability of meeting rooms and other physical assets, the collaboration of churches can make the difference between the success and failure of a homosexual organizational activity."[35]

To offer but one final example, Monsignor William B. Smith has astutely observed that the threat of secularization within Catholic hospitals and health care facilities recently has been greatly exacerbated, in part, through mergers and joint ventures with non-Catholic institutions, and, in part, through the rationalizations provided by dissenting Catholic moral theologians.[36] To the question, "can a Catholic hospital properly be the sponsor or part owner of a joint venture that governs and delivers 'services' that Catholic moral teaching prohibits (e.g., direct abortion, direct sterilization, assisted suicide)?" he responds in the negative: "a Catholic institution cannot sponsor or co-sponsor what it says it is conscientiously opposed to."[37] As he elaborates, "in a joint institutional venture, a full merger, a limited cosponser, co-owner or limited partner, from the viewpoint of corporate governance, the Religious Order or Catholic group that formally and freely established such a joint venture cannot pretend they do not set policy. They do; that's what governance is."[38] Furthermore, Monsignor Smith tellingly suggests that "with beds reduced, with continued reductions in all institutions, with a greatly lessened presence of dedicated religious, perhaps the time has come not to play a subordinate role in a secularized system but seek more limited but real services to those in need now and surely in the future: the unborn; pregnancy care; those whose quality-of-life won't rate in reimbursement schemes (for-profit or governmental); and those disorganized folks 'freed' from institutions but wandering the streets in a daze."[39]

Gerard Morrissey summarizes all of this well:

> While the current attack by "Catholic dissenters" on the Church's teaching is basically the same as the past attack by non-Catholics, it is considerably more painful. A betrayal from within your own family hurts more than the fiercest onslaught from without. In addition, when the attack comes from outside, it is much easier to set up defenses to shield yourself. Until recently, Catholic schools and newspapers could be relied upon for this purpose. Today...these very institutions have often fallen into the hands of dissenters. Instead of being instruments of defense, they are now instruments of attack. Instead of building up, they now destroy.[40]

What makes all of these examples of a "secularization from within" so insidious is precisely the legitimacy wrongly afforded to such developments by a purposely twisted interpretation of the Faith. A Church so internally divided can barely stand, never mind transform the American public square with an authentic Catholic presence.

Notes

1. Peter L. Berger, *The Sacred Canopy: Elements of a Sociological Theory of Religion* (New York: Doubleday and Company, 1967).
2. Joseph A. Varacalli, *Toward the Establishment of Liberal Catholicism in America* (Lanham, Maryland: University Press of America, 1983), 115.
3. Varacalli, *Toward the Establishment*, 189. Joseph A. Varacalli, "The State of the American Catholic Laity: Propositions and Proposals," *Faith and Reason* 13, no. 2 (summer 1987): 126-166.
4. Julia Mitchell Corbett, *Religion in America* (Englewood Cliffs, New Jersey: Prentice-Hall, 1994), 142.
5. J. Brian Benestad, *The Pursuit of a Just Social Order: Policy Statements of the U.S. Catholic Bishops, 1966-80* (Washington, D.C.: Ethics and Public Policy Center, 1982).
6. George Weigel, *Tranquillitas Ordinis: The Present Failure and Future Promise of American Catholic Thought on War and Peace* (Oxford: Oxford University Press, 1987).
7. Monsignor George A. Kelly, *Keeping the Church Catholic with John Paul II* (New York: Doubleday, 1990), 134.
8. Kelly, *Keeping the Church*, 134.
9. Kelly, *Keeping the Church*, 134.
10. Kelly, *Keeping the Church*, 136.
11. James K. Fitzpatrick, "Was Leo XIII a Liberal Democrat?" *Wanderer* (9 May 1996), 9.
12. Father Avery Dulles, S.J., *Religion and the Transformation of Politics* (New York: Fordham University Press, 1993), 5-6.
13. Monsignor Kelly, *Keeping the Church*, 142.

14. Monsignor Kelly, *Keeping the Church*, 138.

15. Monsignor Kelly, *Keeping the Church*, 142.

16. Monsignor Kelly, *Keeping the Church*, 157.

17. Monsignor Kelly, *Keeping the Church*, 163-164.

18. Monsignor Kelly, *Keeping the Church*, 186.

19. Michael Warner, *Changing Witness: Catholic Bishops and Public Policy, 1917-1994* (Washington, D.C.: Ethics and Public Policy Center, 1995), 167-168.

20. Warner, *Changing Witness*, 170.

21. Rev. Andrew M. Greeley, *The Communal Catholic* (New York: Seabury, 1976), 2-3.

22. Joseph A. Varacalli, "The Failure of the Therapeutic: Implications for Society and Church," *Faith and Reason* 23, no. 1 (spring 1997): 3-22.

23. William Kirk Kilpatrick, *Psychological Seduction: The Failure of Modern Psychology* (Nashville, Tennessee: Thomas Nelson Publishers, 1983), 14.

24. James O'Kane, "A Sociological View of U.S. Catholicism," in *Teaching the Catholic Faith: Central Questions for the 90s*, Monsignor Eugene V. Clark, ed. (New York: St. John's University Press, 1991).

25. Monsignor Michael Wrenn, *Catechisms and Controversies: Religious Education in the Postconciliar Years* (San Francisco, California: Ignatius Press, 1991), 80-81.

26. James Hitchcock, *The Pope and the Jesuits* (New York: The National Committee of Catholic Laymen, 1984), 23.

27. William Coulson, "Repentent Psychologist: How I Wrecked the I.H.M. Nuns," interview conducted by Dr. William Marra, *The Latin Mass: Chronicles of a Catholic Reform* (Special Issue, 1994).

28. Gerard Morrissey, *The Crisis of Dissent* (Front Royal, Virginia: Christendom Publications, 1985), 11-12.

29. Joseph A. Varacalli, "'Homophobia' at Seton Hall University: Sociology in Defense of the Faith," *Faith and Reason* 20, no. 3 (fall 1994): 281-307. Joseph A. Varacalli, "Secular Sociology's War against *Familiaris Consortio* and the Traditional Family: Whither Catholic Higher Education and Catholic Sociology?" in *The Church and the Universal Catechism*, Rev. Anthony J. Mastroeni, ed. (Steubenville, Ohio: Franciscan University Press, 1992).

30. Philip Gleason, *Contending with Modernity: Catholic Higher Education in the Twentieth Century* (Oxford: Oxford University Press, 1995), 305.

31. Gleason, *Contending with Modernity*, 322.

32. Monsignor George A. Kelly, "Catholic Higher Education: Is It in or out of the Church?" *Faith and Reason* 18, no. 1 (spring 1992): 44.

33. Joseph A. Varacalli, "Obstructing *Ex corde Ecclesiae*," *Faith and Reason* 23, nos. 3-4 (1997-98): 369-386.

34. Paul Likoudis, "Experts Agree: It's Time for Bishops to Pull Their Heads from the Sand," *Wanderer* (27 March 1997): 1, 5.

35. Rev. Enrique Rueda and Michael Schwartz, *Gays, AIDS, and You* (Old Greenwich, Connecticut: The Devin Adair Company, 1987), 85, 91.

36. Monsignor William B. Smith, "Questions Answered: Cooperation Revisited," *Homiletic and Pastoral Review* 97, no. 4 (January 1997): 67-69.

37. Monsignor William B. Smith, "Questions Answered: Cooperation in Health Care," *Homiletic and Pastoral Review* 96, no. 10 (June 1996): 72.

38. Monsignor Smith, "Cooperation in Health Care," 71.

39.   Monsignor Smith, "Cooperation in Health Care," 72.
40.   Morrissey, *Crisis*, 16.

Chapter Ten

A Failure in Vision and Nerve: The Present Accommodation of "Americanist" Catholic Leadership

It is unnerving to admit that God only knows too well how widespread lies the blame for the present unsatisfactory condition of the Catholic Church in the United States. All have all failed Christ, in some way or another and to some degree, this author most definitely included. Having acknowledged this, reason also reaffirms the truthfulness of Harry Truman's statement about the ultimate responsibility that is part and parcel of any top organizational leadership position, to wit, that "the buck stops here." In the case at hand, the buck stops with the bishops of the United States, both collectively through the National Conference of Catholic Bishops/United States Catholic Conference or individually through their exercise of authority in the dioceses in which they lead. Simply put, too many bishops have dropped the buck. Instead of leading their flocks along the righteous path, they themselves have turned sheepish in their duties. Indeed as the then-Prefect of the Congregation for the Doctrine of the Faith, Cardinal Francis Seper, put it in 1972:

> The bishops, who obtained many powers for themselves at the Council, are often to blame because in this crisis they are not exercising their powers as they should. Rome is too far away to cope with every scandal—and Rome is not well obeyed. If all the bishops would deal decisively with these aberrations as they occur, the situation would be different. It is very difficult for us in Rome if we get no cooperation from the bishops.[1]

Why there is this failure in leadership and lack of cooperation with legitimate Roman Catholic authorities is a fascinating question that escapes a fully satisfactory answer. However, there are some partial pieces of the puzzle that can be put together. They are, respectively, *demographic* and *historical, social-structural, ideational, cultural* and *characterological.*

One factor is partly *demographic,* partly the result of an unhappy *historical* and prudential judgment made by Pope Paul VI. Demographically, most of those solidly orthodox bishops who presided over the Church during its height in post-World War II America have either passed away or retired. In and by itself, this development is insignificant. Unfortunately, it takes on great significance when one understands the nature of the younger generation that replaced them. Pope Paul VI apparently placed great reliance on the judgment of his American Apostolic Delegate, the Belgian Archbishop, Jean Jadot.[2] Archbishop Jadot recommended numerous younger candidates for bishop; many were fully prepared to preside over a Catholic accommodation to the secularism found outside of the Church and were ready to acquiesce to the secularism found within. Monsignor George A. Kelly notes that "a case can be made that Apostolic delegate Jean Jadot, Rome's bishop maker in the U.S. between 1973 and 1980, contributed over one hundred bishops to the American scene, some of whom were in sympathy with the new theology and pluralistic forms the Church was adopting"[3] and for "which he earned high marks from the Church's 'progressive' forces."[4] For this breed, it was definitely a left-leaning sign of the times interpretation of Church and society that was embraced. These bishops, young priests in the mid-1960s and 1970s, are now middle-aged and at the height of their power and influence. They now represent a bottleneck against the sentiments of the present cohort of many younger and recently appointed bishops promoted to the episcopate during the pontificate of John Paul II. While taken as a group and viewed from the perspective of orthodoxy, the John Paul II group represents a marked improvement; however, the improvement is not as startling and clear-cut as one might expect. Why less than fully orthodox bishops have been appointed during John Paul II's reign is somewhat of a mystery. Intelligent speculations might include the present pontiff's respect for the position of the senior bishops of America who promote, predictably enough, their own kind; to the generation of "stealth" candidates who are made to appear other than what they really are; or to a kind of "practical" political bargaining between Rome and leading Americanists.

A second factor that helps to explain the failed vision and nerve of American Catholic ecclesiastical leadership is more *social-structural* in nature, which holds constant the philosophy of the individual bishop in question. One aspect of this is the hold (perhaps, in many cases, more perceived than real) that a dissident clergy has over their ecclesiastical superior. Analogous to the generational movement among American bishops is one among the priesthood. As older more orthodox priests pass from the scene in one way or another, the once "new breed" generation of priests moves into the powerful positions of the Church bureaucracy, again placing a cap on the upward movement and influence of the latest crop of, once again, younger, more orthodox clergy. Apparently, even many orthodox bishops feel that this dissident bloc is a social fact of life that must be respected politically (if not religiously).

Another social-structural aspect is the changing social status of the Catholic lay community. As Monsignor George A. Kelly astutely observed in 1982:

> ...the colorful "characters" in the hierarchy of a generation or two ago had one advantage over modern bishops: as outsiders in a Protestant culture, they did not have to worry about popularity or acceptance. They could proclaim their faith even if it annoyed native Americans, confident that they were rallying points for Catholics. Today, however, bishops have a social status of a different kind. They are integrated leaders within...[an] American community...wedded more to civil religion than to confessional bodies. The Catholic community itself has been secularized and is comfortable with bishops who follow the leadership-style in modern society. It no longer is one in its beliefs, nor disposed anymore to rally around bishops simply because they are bishops.[5]

Yet another social-structural consideration retarding the implementation of an authentic Catholic vision is presented by Gerard Morrissey. He argues that some bishops who are orthodox and vitally concerned with issues of doctrine nonetheless have not adjusted to the reality that, in the post-Vatican II era, Church bureaucracies are no longer manned by loyal administrators but by a new Catholic knowledge class promoting dissent. For Morrissey

> [the] situation has now changed radically. Instead of being loyal to the Church's teaching, many of the specialists are now far more loyal to the dissenters or to their own ideas. Nevertheless, despite the fact that a new pattern has emerged, the personal actions of most bishops still presume that the old pattern continues to exist and that the defense of Church teachings will be taken care of by specialists while the bishops will concentrate on the administrative and the practical....[the] bishops pass fine statements in support of Church teaching but they leave the implementation of these statements to specialists who disagree with what they have said.[6]

Another factor lies in the realm of *ideas*, more specifically, in the acceptance of a false and heterodox understanding of pluralism both inside and outside of the Church. There has, of course, always been pluralism within the Church. The key analytical question, however, is whether the pluralistic option (in theology, devotional style, religious order affiliation, national or ethnic cultural attachment, among others) coheres with, enlivens, and energizes a Magisterially defined Catholic faith. Empirically, many forms of pluralism are successful in this regard; evangelization and inculturation are not intended to be antithetical to each other. Many times, however, pluralism masks the reality that an individual's or group's ultimate source of authority is something other than the Faith, correctly understood. The relevance of this for the issue at hand is that many bishops are, in the final analysis, actually propelled into action by some other than authentically Catholic allegiance, whether it be the present larger American culture, feminism, Marxism, ethnicity, or the therapeutic or new age mentalities. The Catholic faith, in this case, is certainly referred to for the sake of legitimization, but the Faith is actually cut down to selectively fit the needs of the ideology in question. Put another way, the "communal Catholicism" that Rev. Greeley celebrates among the American Catholic population at large is, unfortunately, also a reality for top ecclesiastical leadership, (although, with the exception of a few shameless bishops, is not as likely to be publicly celebrated).[7]

Related to changes in ideas is the issue of the stance of American Catholics and, more to the point, American Catholic bishops, vis-à-vis the broader American *culture*. As is well known, during the turn of the last century the Catholic Church in the United States was marked by a titanic struggle between two factions. Using Rev. Andrew M. Greeley's terminology, the first or "Americanizer" faction argued that Catholics ought not view American culture and society as in any major way antithetical to the Catholic religion.[8] The second or conservative camp argued that the full assimilation of Catholics into American thought and life was fraught with dangers to the Faith. In 1899, Pope Leo XIII intervened by issuing his encyclical, *Testem benevolentiae*, which focused on the "heresy of Americanism." In the encyclical, the pope admonished Catholics about certain attitudes and practices opposed to Catholicism. These included the tendencies to (1) assert the superiority of "active" over "passive" virtues, (2) assert the superiority of the "natural" to the "supernatural," and (3) reduce the faith to surrounding culture. The latter tendency included both external and internal dimensions. By the former, external dimension, the pope meant what orthodox Catholics would today call a false ecumenism in which the Church herself is co-opted by the visions of other religions and secular worldviews. By the latter, internal dimension, the pope meant the idea of a radical democratization within the Church that would, for all intents and purposes, eliminate the central and constitutively Catholic guardian role performed by the Magisterium.

Unsurprisingly, the Americanizer and anti-Americanizer factions interpreted the relevance of *Testem benevolentiae* quite differently. As recorded by the progressive Church historian Monsignor John Tracy Ellis:

> Following the publication of the Pope's letter, the bishops of the Provinces of Milwaukee and New York thanked Leo XIII for saving the American Church from heresy. The more common reaction in the United States, however, was that embodied in the reply of Cardinal Gibbons to the pontiff on March 17, 1899, when he said, "This doctrine, which I deliberately call extravagant and absurd, this Americanism as it had been called, has nothing in common with the views, aspirations, doctrine, and conduct of...[Catholic] Americans."[9]

Regardless of whether or not the turn of the twentieth century "heresy of Americanism" was a phantom or not—I'm inclined to agree with Dennis P. McCann that it wasn't[10]—the issue of a heretical "Americanism" in the *contemporary* Catholic Church of the United States has never been so real. It is, more to the point, an Americanism that has infected more than a few of America's present crop of bishops. In retrospect, one can plausibly argue that the publication of *Testem benevolentiae*, "On the Heresy of Americanism" (1899), and *Pascendi Dominici Gregis*, "On the Modernist Heresy" (1907), sociologically held in check the secularizing orientation of the Americanist impulse until a highly distorted and selective interpretation of Vatican II in the post-Vatican era unleashed its self-liquidating impulses. I have previously argued that there are at least six contemporary "constitutive elements" of the idea of an "American" Catholic Church.[11] They are (1) a highly optimistic understanding of the present religious state of affairs, (2) an almost symmetrical understanding of the relationship between prevailing culture and existing faith, (3) an exaggerated sense of the importance of secular intellectual disciplines, (4) either an "altruistic" or highly "malleable" understanding of human nature, (5) an image of God as either "remote" or as "lover," and (6) an understanding of the institutional Church that emphasizes its human, finite, and socially constructed side, which pronounces its inability to grasp fundamental truth better than any other agency or individual, and which argues its dispensability for anything but a mission to institutionalize a this-worldly social justice along socialistic lines and to meet the personal therapeutic needs of the individual.

Finally, there is the *characterological* issue of the personality make-up of individual bishops. Some have strong personalities but lack vision. Some are holy but lack discernment. Some are, simply, weak. Some are too concerned with being "popular." Some are too career oriented to buck the dominant Cardinals "Dearden-Bernardin" wing of the Church that controls much of the distribution of power, status, and jobs within the Church in America. Some have themselves embraced secular fads and, as such, represent high level "communal Catholics." And, following St. Paul, a few might very well represent an out-and-out apostasy working, consciously or not, for the powers and principalities, "the spiritual hosts of wickedness in the heavenly places" (Eph. 6:12).

These various demographic, historical, social-structural, ideational, cultural, and characterological factors partially can be accommodated analytically in the useful typology of "Four Categories of Bishops" offered by Gerard Morrissey.[12] Morrissey's first category is "Knowledge—Acceptance—No Action." As he continues, these "bishops know about the problem of dissent but do not act because, either openly or tacitly, they approve of dissent, or at least consider dissent to be an acceptable option for Catholics."[13] This is followed by the category, "No Knowledge—No Acceptance—No Action." For the author, these "bishops do not act because they are not aware (or at least not fully aware) of all the things the dissenters are doing."[14] The third category is "Knowledge—No Acceptance—But No Action." In this case, "the bishops know about the problem, do not approve dissent, but do not act because they believe (a) they are powerless; (b) they would look foolish if they attempted to check dissent; (c) attempts to check dissent would only boomerang and create more sympathy for those opposing the Pope; (d) attempts to check dissent would be a *pastoral* mistake (i.e., it would lead to a tremendous institutional upheaval against the bishop with an open revolt very likely...a deliberate decision by the bishop to ignore the problem prevents an open revolt and brings about a surface peace); and (e) avoidance of the problem must be the best policy since it is what the other bishops are doing."[15] Morrissey's final category is "Knowledge—No Acceptance—Some Action." In these cases, "the bishops know about the problem and do not approve of dissent, but they believe they are taking effective action (a) by their own personal statements in support of Church teachings; and (b) by efforts that take place 'behind the scenes.'"[16]

All of these considerations plus others, both natural and supernatural, have produced what, *in general*, must be considered a weak and ineffectual ecclesiastical leadership in the United States. The results are horrendous: a Church in which most are doctrinal illiterates; do not satisfactorily participate in the sacramental system and devotions of the Church; are religiously deaf to the reality of, and demands for entrance into, Heaven; are incapable of authentically interpreting the significance of religious experience; and lack the social consciousness that can only be fully nurtured by understanding, accepting, and following Catholic morality and Catholic social teaching.

Monsignor George A. Kelly's 1982 assessment of "the misguided leadership of American Bishops" is almost as valid today as then:

> The Body of American Bishops, not this or that bishop, has failed to provide the governance needed for the Church during the period of radical change following the Second Vatican Council. Had any other institution but the Catholic Church suffered such declines and divisions, the top management personnel would now have been reshuffled and the institution itself reorganized. There is a permanency of appointment, however, for Catholic bishops sanctioned by tradition which makes it unlikely that many of them, if any, will be fired for inefficiency or incompetent leadership.[17]

Nonetheless, the appointments to the office of bishop made by John Paul II during his pontificate have, incrementally at least, improved the quality of high-level decision-making in the Catholic Church in the United States. Such a transformation is a necessary, albeit not sufficient, condition for an authentic Catholic moment to emerge.

Notes

1. Gerard Morrissey, *The Crisis of Dissent* (Front Royal, Virginia: Christendom Publications, 1985), 11.
2. Rev. Andrew M. Greeley, *The American Catholic* (New York: Basic Books, 1977). Monsignor George A. Kelly, *Keeping the Church Catholic with John Paul II* (New York: Doubleday, 1990).
3. Monsignor Kelly, *Keeping the Church*, 143.

4. Monsignor George A. Kelly, *The Battle for the Church Revisited* (San Francisco, California: Ignatius Press, 1995), 41.

5. Monsignor George A. Kelly, *The Crisis of Authority: John Paul II and the American Bishops* (Chicago, Illinois: Regnery Gateway, 1982), 58.

6. Morrissey, *Crisis*, 113.

7. Rev. Andrew M. Greeley, *The Communal Catholic* (New York: Seabury, 1976).

8. Rev. Andrew M. Greeley, *The Catholic Experience* (New York: Doubleday, 1967).

9. Monsignor John Tracy Ellis, *Documents of American Catholic History*, Monsignor John Tracy Ellis, ed. (Milwaukee, Wisconsin: Bruce Publishing, 1956), 533.

10. Dennis P. McCann, *New Experiment in Democracy: The Challenge for American Catholicism* (Kansas City, Missouri: Sheed and Ward, 1987). Joseph A. Varacalli, "Book Review of Dennis P. McCann's *New Experiment in Democracy*," *Homiletic and Pastoral Review* 88, no. 10 (July 1988): 72-74.

11. Joseph A. Varacalli, "The Constitutive Elements of the Idea of an 'American' Catholic Church," *Social Justice Review* 80, nos. 5-6 (May-June 1989): 85-91.

12. Morrissey, *Crisis*, 100-101.

13. Morrissey, 100.

14. Morrissey, 100.

15. Morrissey, 100-101.

16. Morrissey, 101.

17. Monsignor Kelly, *Crisis of Authority*, 73.

Chapter Eleven

First Things First: Catholic Participation in Secular America

The primary mission of the Catholic Church is the salvation of souls. Likewise, at the individual level, the ultimate destiny of each human being is not to acquire worldly "success" but to reach heaven. This is expressed beautifully in St. Augustine's prayer and acknowledgment to God in his *Confessions* that, for Christians, "our hearts are restless until they rest in Thee." The Church, seeing herself as both a divine and human institution, saves souls through the administration of the sacraments, through the celebration of a divine liturgy and devotional life, through teaching doctrine to her members, through evangelization efforts, and through the exercise and exemplification of her social apostolate.

The Catholic Imperative in Politics and Civil Life

Regarding the social apostolate, eternal salvation for the individual requires not merely demonstrated activity in good works and charity but the attempted institutionalization in society of social justice, properly understood. As the 1971 statement, *Justice in the World*, declared, "a concern for social justice...is a *constitutive* feature of the preaching of the Gospel" (italics added). "Constitutive," however, must not be confused with "definitive"; herein lies one important incongruity between orthodox Catholicism and the vision of secularists and most present day "liberationist" and "Americanist" thinking.[1]

85

The social reconstruction of society along authentic Christian lines, while *a good in and by itself*, is, nonetheless, not the raison d'être of the Catholic faith. Rather, it is a lesser good; it is both secondary to and derivative of the primary mission of assisting individuals in the quest for eternal, otherworldly salvation. In the final analysis, from a Catholic perspective, individuals are seen stumbling to the cross in a this-worldly "vale of tears." But as we stumble we are also commissioned by Christ to do so in solidarity with, and with concern for, all of His children and for all of His human creation, the political and civil order included.

Another important incongruity between Catholic and non-Catholic thinking lies in the set of principles utilized in the attempted reconstruction of the social order. From an orthodox Catholic perspective, neither the socialism of the cultural and economic Left or the capitalism of the economic Right contain the necessary kit of useful and right-ordered principles. Put another way, such Catholic principles as "subsidiarity" and "personalism" cross-cut and are not isomorphic with either the totalism of socialism or the autonomous individualism of capitalism. The "restoration of all things in Christ," society included, naturally presupposes the institutionalization of the Church's social doctrine. Put another way, Catholic participation in America presupposes that first things must come first. One must be Catholic before one is American. To put this more "acceptably," perhaps one can state that one can be truly American by authentically fulfilling one's mandate to the Faith.

Idolatries: Old and New

Catholic social theory does not support any version of "angelism." As an incarnational religion, Catholicism acknowledges that our souls are inextricably intertwined in bodies, that grace works through nature, that reason is embedded within a matrix of emotions and other nonrational attachments, and that individuals are necessarily and intimately affected by cultural and socialization influences that are temporally and spatially bound. The spirit, in essence, must continually be in a critically self-conscious relationship with both human nature and society if it is to master, or at least reasonably control, these relationships. And, obviously, it is clear that, in far too many cases, the spirit is subdued both by nature and society.

Put another way, the primary social-scientific explanation for the present day plethora of heterodoxies from an authentic exercise of the Catholic faith on the part of nominal/dormant Catholics involves the inevitable human reality of mediation. That is, the Catholic Faith is mediated through some distinctive personality orientation or some cultural construction (e.g., nationality, ethnicity, socioeconomic class affiliation, philosophy, or ideology) that is capable of producing a radically individualistic or communal Catholicism. In these instances, the Catholic Faith is understood as a secondary allegiance that is selectively absorbed into some other moral commitment considered ultimately more significant.[2]

In the case of Catholic orthodoxy, it is the Catholic Faith, as defined by Magisterial authority, that serves as the leaven for culture, history, the individual, and nature. The issue of the inevitability of cultural mediation was at the heart of the "Americanist controversy" at the turn of the last century that has resurfaced with a vengeance in the post-Vatican II period of the Church in the United States. Theoretically, if not empirically, neither the "Americanizers," that is, those who wanted Catholics to immerse themselves quickly into American society nor the "anti-Americanizers," that is, those who wanted to maintain their Catholicism through their national (e.g., German, Polish, French) cultures had the better of the argument. The idolatrous possibilities of submerging and making subordinate the Faith to culture existed in either case. Interestingly enough, however, many—although not all—of the modern-day descendants of the Americanists today champion the cause of a radical "cultural and religious pluralism" while most of the latter descendants of the anti-Americanizers defend Rome and Magisterial teaching.[3]

The point that must be stressed, however, is that in those cases in which the Catholic faith does *not* maintain a hold over culture and nature, heterodoxy is the inevitable result. Heterodoxy, furthermore, can take either "pagan" or "neo-pagan" form. Paganism results from those cases in which some *premodern* cultural formation (e.g., the family, village) takes priority over Catholicism. Neo-paganism emerges in those cases in which some *modern* cultural formation (e.g., the nation-state, "new age" thinking, the corporation) replaces Catholicism as central in consciousness. Given that neo-paganism more often entails a more self-conscious rejection of an already well-established Catholic alternative, it involves greater culpability and sinfulness than does paganism, per se. And while the modern, "post-Christian" era is more likely to contain neo-pagan, as compared to pagan, forms of heterodoxy, paganistic expressions are far from empirically unavailable. Recent studies completed on the contemporary religiosity of Italian Americans indicate that both paganistic and neo-paganistic expressions coexist alongside of authentic Catholic manifestations and sensibilities.[4] In addition to an authentic veneration of the saints in the famous "giglio feast" of Brooklyn, New York, for instance, one can find abundant evidence of "old world" superstitions, magic, and other non-Catholic cultural practices as well as contemporary secular ideological commitments to American patriotism, upward social mobility, Italian-American ethnicity, and a general sense of "Italianita."[5]

A Presently Hostile Climate

Anti-Catholicism, to quote the felicitous phrase of Michael Schwartz, has constituted a "persistent prejudice" throughout American history.[6] Originally, the source of this prejudice derived from the hegemonic status—culturally, economically, and politically—of a generic Protestantism. Today, as a formerly society-defining liberal Protestantism has completed the process of digging its own grave, American civilization is now given articulation and shape within the American public sphere megastructural institutions of government, the corporation, the academy, the mass media, Hollywood, and popular art and music by an almost pristine version of secularism. This secularism is at least as virulently anti-Catholic as was American Protestant culture. It is probably fair to state that the only period of time in which anti-Catholic sentiments abated somewhat was in and around the years of World War II up until the onset of the antinomianism of the 1960s.

While an adequate analysis of just how hostile the present climate in America is for an authentic Catholicism is beyond the scope of this monograph, a few illustrations are in order. Regarding government, the present occupant of the executive branch has just about declared open and unconditional war on the Faith. President William Clinton's unabashedly pro-homosexual and pro-abortion-on-demand actions; his Supreme Court, other judiciary, and high-level cabinet appointments; his hostility to Catholic and private education; and his overtly statist policies are just a few indications that his worldview is fundamentally at odds with a Catholic/Judaic-Christian worldview. Note should be taken of Stephen M. Krason's argument that the single most effective political means of reversing the present trend in the culture war is to elect a strong and orthodox Catholic president of the United States who is not afraid to utilize the broad and sweeping powers of the office.[7]

That the judiciary branch is also overtly hostile to the Judaic-Christian heritage was made clear through a symposium published in the November 1996 issue of *First Things* and subsequently debated and elaborated on in many forums.[8] Titled "The End of Democracy?: The Judicial Usurpation of Politics," it contained contributions by editor-in-chief Rev. Richard J. Neuhaus and scholars Robert H. Bork, Russell Hittinger, Hadley Arkes, Charles W. Colson, and Robert P. George. The overall thesis presented was that the judiciary is progressively usurping the authority granted in the American constitutional order to the citizenry—through debate, elections, and representative political institutions—to decide upon the ultimate questions confronting the Republic. Russell Shaw summarizes well the overall thrust of the symposium:

> For the *First Things* writers, as for other conservatives, the prime examples of judicial overreaching are the Supreme Court's abortion decisions, starting with *Roe vs. Wade* in 1973 and continuing through *Planned Parenthood vs. Casey* in 1992. Also high on the list are 1996 Supreme Court decisions overturning a voter approved ban on preferential treatment for homosexuals in Colorado and

requiring the venerable Virginia Military Institute to admit women. Other instances include federal-court decisions last year striking down New York and Washington laws against assisted suicide...and a December...[1996] ruling by a Hawaii court saying the state must recognize homosexual "marriages." Conservative outrage in the face of such court decisions is hardly new. What was new in the case of the *First Things* symposium was the radical nature of the critique, which questioned whether the "regime" created in the United States still commanded the support of conscientious citizens.[9]

A second theme in the *First Things Symposium*, expressed especially by Robert George in a contribution that took as its main reference John Paul II's *Evangelium Vitae*, was that all law must be evaluated in light of universal standards of justice. That the natural law, in various ways, should, but at this moment doesn't sufficiently, influence judicial decision making was the subject of a "Symposium on Natural Law in American Politics and Constitutional Law" published in the premier issue of *The Catholic Social Science Review*, for which Robert George wrote a useful introduction.[10] For William Bentley Ball and Stephen M. Krason, for instance, judges must appeal beyond the positive law of the Constitution to the natural law to invalidate legislation that is unjust. Given that, periodically, sound constitutional law depends completely upon sound unrestricted moral reasoning, the positive law of the American Constitution, for Gerard V. Bradley, can and must occasionally make appeals to the natural law. And, finally, David Forte argues that those judges operating under natural law norms will inevitably manifest more respect for the idea of judicial restraint.[11]

It is only in one of the two branches of Congress, that is, in the House of Representatives, that one can say that the Judaic-Christian (although not specifically Catholic) worldview occasionally receives a respectful hearing. This is due, undoubtedly, to the reality that House members are structurally closer to (and hence, more accountable to) a public that is still somewhat tied to the Judaic-Christian heritage than is a more elitist, "gnostic-like," Senate.

Corporate America, for its part, consciously fosters a consumerist spirit at odds with the authentic religious spirit. Moreover, it fails to even produce its materialist dream for all Americans as the bottom line is efficiency in order to maximize corporate profits. The result is a corporate culture unconcerned with the dignity of the individual as manifested by dramatic increases in layoffs and part-time employment and losses in a host of worker's benefits. Even when occasionally articulated by a now emaciated Catholic intellectual presence in American public policy circles, calls for a "living wage" to strengthen the nuclear family and to support the wife's necessary role in the nurturance of young children go unheeded. In both big ways and small, the educational establishment, from kindergarten through college, works to foster a secular worldview and, conversely, to attack the fundamental role of religion in American society, with a special animus directed against Catholicism. For instance, character development and the belief that there is an objective truth and moral order is eschewed by educational "experts" in favor of preaching either moral relativism[12] or some quite specific and politically correct utopianism (e.g., socialism, feminism).[13] This takes place under the guise of implementing such approaches as "multiculturalism,"[14] "value-free" human sexuality courses, and, in general, all "experiential" educational approaches as fostered by the modern day devotees of John Dewey.

Representatives of both conservative thought[15] and the radical Left[16] argue that an almost hegemonic mass media is not objective in its news reporting but is saturated by uncritically accepted mainstream liberal values. In the case of the radical Left, the mass media is seen to serve as a propaganda mill in the service of a wealthy and powerful corporate America. In the case of conservatives and orthodox Catholic thinkers, the mass media is seen as a vehicle to institutionalize the autonomous individualism of the new class, which almost invariably translates into expressions that range from utopian to morally relativistic to nihilistic in nature.

One could profitably apply the previous analysis in the Introduction of how values affect the social scientific enterprise to journalistic and all other forms of "rational" thinking, from that of the professional social activist to that of the average citizen. Simply put, the fact that America's media elite are far to the left of the American public opinion on the great majority of public issues[17] including, of course, abortion, *does* translate into pervasive liberal biases, both overt and subtle. Put another way, such issues, among others, as motivation, topic selection, tacit philosophy embraced, language chosen, evidence accepted, and mode of interpretation intimately color the journalistic enterprise. The simple solution to this scandal would be the infusion of "other-than-liberal" journalists into the profession. The more profound solution, of course, would require a cultural revolution in the worldview of intellectuals, mass media experts, and other public sphere participants in the direction of an acceptance and acknowledgment of the natural law.

That the existing Hollywood movie industry and the contemporary worlds of art and music constantly mock anything that smacks of tradition is now, unfortunately, a taken-for-granted reality. And it is a taken-for-granted reality that can be easily empirically tested by comparing representative movies, art, and music from the 1950s through to the present. Perverted human relationships, unnatural forms of sexual behavior, and excessive violence for "shock value" are now too commonly the norm in these venues.

With all too few exceptions, then, the public sphere of American life is openly hostile to the Judaic-Christian and, especially, the Catholic worldview. Given that it is the public sphere that gives overall articulation and form to American life—that defines a society's "official" understanding of itself—the issue remains as to "what should be the political and social response of authentic and loyal Catholics to an American social order becoming progressively more secular."

Repairing the American Social Order or Rebuilding It on a Catholic Foundation?

Earlier in this volume, I had spoken of "the pyrrhic victory of individualism in American civilization: the exhaustion of an inadequate idea." The thesis then presented downplayed the argument made by scholars like Rev. John Courtney Murray[18] to the effect that the roots of the American Republic were *effectively* grounded in the principles of the natural law. More precisely, I argued the ineffectiveness of the natural law for two reasons: (1) the natural law that infused the original vision of American society was diluted by Deist, Enlightenment influences and (2) more importantly, the effectiveness of the natural law depends significantly on the compatibility of its cultural mediator, which in American civilization has been either Protestantism or secularism. Conversely put, my argument is consistent with the theme made by scholars like John Rao[19] to the effect that American civilization is, at bottom, a Protestant idea whose focal point is much more the value of individualism than anything akin to the natural law.[20] Early in its history, individualism in American life was both contained and given centrifugal direction toward the idea of a Good Society primarily by a Protestant biblical and, secondarily, by a deist republican, vision. As Robert Bellah and his colleagues, among others, have noted, individualism in American society has now become privatized, and I would add, selfish, as the value of individualism is primarily operationalized, in the American middle classes, to promote success in the sphere of work ("utilitarian individualism") and in the spheres of inter- and intrapersonal development ("expressive individualism").[21] Part and parcel of this movement, whose ultimate endpoint is the idea of "autonomous individualism," is the ascendancy of moral relativism in both belief and practice. Put another way, the claim of a Catholic restorationist critique is that our present day run-amok individualism, relativism, hedonism, and narcissism are the logical result of the internal contradictions of Protestantism in American civilization working themselves out in history.

It follows from my analysis that changes in the meaning of individualism affect the degree to which it is easy or hard for the average citizen to apprehend the natural law, which is, nonetheless, written into the heart. Contemporary forms of individualism make it easy for the natural law to be perverted into a bogus "natural rights" perspective in which individuals today claim "rights" to abortion and assisted suicide, among other pathologies. David Blankenhorn unintentionally demonstrates how the natural law, as embodied in this country's Declaration of Independence and surrounded by the cultural value of individualism, can be perverted into a "right to divorce":

> For the idea of better divorce, while certainly not confined to the United States, is so prevalent in this nation precisely because its roots run so deep in

American history and in what might be termed the larger American narrative. The vision of the good divorce—a vision of personal freedom—captures much of the essence of the American character. Our nation's founding document is a divorce document. It is a declaration of independence: an enumeration of the reasons for which people may justifiably dissolve the bonds that have connected them to others. In no other nation is the idea of "starting over" invested with such optimism and hope.[22]

The question now surfaces as to whether the proper goal of orthodox Catholicism is merely to repair the social fabric—bringing it back to, say, the condition of the 1950s—or to fundamentally restructure a decaying American civilization along lines derived from the social doctrine of the Church. The restorationist answer offered here is clearly the latter, for the logic of liberalism eventually would surely dissolve any attempted new Christendom as it dissolved the Catholic world of the immediate post-World War II generation. It is liberalism that ultimately must be replaced; hence my rejection of the foundational viewpoint of such prominent Catholic neoconservatives as Michael Novak, George Weigel, and Rev. Richard J. Neuhaus. I simply disagree with the recent judgment of Rev. Neuhaus when he categorically states that "there is no going back to reconstitute the American order on a foundation other than the liberal tradition."[23] (For a fascinating debate on this issue, see the ruminations of Robert P. Hunt, Mark Lowery, Adrian Walker, and Kenneth L. Grasso in a recent symposium sponsored and published by the Society of Catholic Social Scientists.)[24]

To reject the underlying neoconservative understanding of the social order as necessarily based on liberalism and individualism is not the same thing, however, as rejecting the neoconservative *method* for promoting a desired form of social change. Simply put, the only practical method for advancing the restorationist agenda is to utilize existing liberal institutions and the democratic process to combat the secular monopoly in the public sphere or, conversely, to restore all things in Christ.[25] As such, I am presently giving no serious consideration to the other logical possibilities facing Catholics in a hostile climate: physically leaving the country, accepting passively in martyrdom the present situation, conducting violent revolution, or withdrawing into sectlike isolation. (The only exception to the above would be the exercise of a responsible "civil disobedience" in the face of the State-sanctioned various "culture of death" activities, e.g., abortion, euthanasia.)

The neoconservative method that I am suggesting as my primary sociological vehicle for social change is noncoercive, civil, allows Catholics to present Catholicism whole and undiluted, and should be viewed as a temporary means to the end of bringing about a new Christendom. If it is successful, that is, as more American citizens are successfully evangelized into the Faith, then a majority of the population might consciously and of free will and good heart desire a civilization based on explicitly Catholic principles. Put crudely, the attempt advocated would be to utilize present-day liberal institutions to dethrone liberalism and individualism and to anoint Catholicism and the natural law. (In such a Catholicized American civilization, all citizens—whether Catholic or not—would be guaranteed the universal rights part and parcel of the natural law; the religious liberty propounded in Vatican II's *Dignitatus Humanae* would be a permanent feature of such a society.)

The neoconservative methodology, following the terminology of Peter L. Berger and the now Rev. Richard J. Neuhaus,[26] is one that transforms the "private sphere" institutions of family, neighborhood, church, and associated voluntary associations into what are called "mediating structures."[27] Like private sphere institutions, mediating structures stand between the isolated individual and the "megastructures" of modern life. Unlike merely private sphere institutions, however, mediating structures are systematically linked and connected to the public sphere. They serve two functions. First, through the democratic processes of modern American life, mediating structures can better represent and protect the individual and subgroup from the concentrated power of either statism or corporate capitalism. Second, they provide the necessary "plausibility structure" or social context that can generate and sustain a worldview at odds with that of the larger culture, thus limiting the otherwise uncontested socializing ability of what the French classical sociologist Emile Durkheim termed the "collective conscience" of society.[28] Mediating structures are intended to counter the political "alienation" and social-psychological "anomie" endemic to all but those out-and-out modernists who fully embrace the values and lifestyle of the secularized public sphere, as well as to oppose the movement by which the "meaning function" is being taken over by non-Catholic agencies.

While Catholic social scientists and social activists who embrace a mediating structures analysis are in agreement that parishes, other Church-related organizations, and other potentially supportive private sphere institutions must be strengthened, they nonetheless can and do disagree over the particulars necessary to bring about this state of affairs. More specifically, there is disagreement over the respective emphasis that ought to be given to the *individual, cultural,* and *structural* levels.

Those who emphasize the *individual* level believe strongly that the initial starting point must be the conversion of the heart. Catholic evangelization and educational efforts geared to the individual will eventually, according to this logic, translate into a converted mainstream culture and strengthened institutional life.

Those who emphasize the *cultural* level believe strongly that a successful Catholic strategy must start by reinfiltrating the key idea-generating sectors of American society, including the government, corporations, mass media, and educational network. Recapturing, or at least neutralizing, these megastructural forces will then, accordingly, reduce the pressure on private sphere institutions and mediating structures, thus freeing the latter to perform their essential

Catholic tasks of evangelization, character development, and responsible participation in civil life.

Those who focus on the *structural* level of institutional life, that is, the building up of the Church's infrastructural network of organizations and of other complementary and positive civil associations, do so because they view this level as a strategic compromise between stressing individual conversion, which is very "doable" but problematic in its ability to create widespread social change in and of itself, and emphasizing widespread cultural change, which would be the effective route to take if it were not so "undoable" without strong institutional support and without intense interest-group pressure in a society in which secular humanism approaches monopoly status in at least key locations.

To start at the structural level, as most proponents of mediating structures would advocate, makes sense in the short run. However, it is vital to note that, to be deemed successful, structural change must quickly translate into success at the individual level and eventually must show gains at the cultural level. At this juncture, several points should be stressed. First of all, the cultural, structural, and individual levels of analysis are interdependent and dialectically related. That is, change at one level will make some impact at other levels. Second, all levels must be addressed simultaneously, although this author would place an initial stress on the structural level for reasons just offered. Finally, there is a natural division of labor, based on differing endowments, personalities, interests, and expertise that should be utilized regarding the respective foci of individual, culture, and social institutions. Simply put, let priests, religious, teachers, and parents proclaim loud and clear the truth of the Catholic religion. Let Catholic social scientists produce Catholic social science and social policy proposals consistent with the faith. Let Catholic social activists organize at both local and national levels. Let Catholic artists produce Catholic art, music, films, and other forms of inspiration and entertainment. Let Christian experts in the various forms of the mass media evangelize their professions. Let Catholic citizens consistently vote for candidates who will not violate the natural law in their governmental roles and activities. A more systematic strategy, however, is called for.

The Two Faces of Mediating Structures: Troeltsch Reconceptualized

As neoconservative thinkers Berger and Neuhaus note, mediating structures have two faces, one directed toward the private sphere, the other toward the public sphere of American life.[29] The two faces of mediating structures, then, suggest a useful distinction regarding the Catholic strategy "to restore all things in Christ." The "internal" approach is geared to the promotion and maintenance of an authentic Catholic worldview by systematically linking, "beefing up," and, when necessary, creating the religious and associated voluntary associations of the private sphere that horizontally surround and can protect and enrich the

Church. Examples here would be organizations like Catholics United for the Faith, Women for Faith and Family, Americans United for the Pope, the Fellowship of Catholic Scholars, the Wanderer Foundation, and the associated activities of Mother Angelica.

The other "external" approach is geared to "taking the battle to the enemy's turf" by, again, connecting, strengthening, and developing organizations that will better represent and help to propagate the Catholic perspective in a public domain that, sociologically, stands above the Church. Examples of organizations here would include the Catholic League for Religious and Civil Rights, the Catholic Campaign for America, and the Society of Catholic Social Scientists, the latter explicitly created, in part, to bring Catholic social doctrine into American public policy. Presently, there is a great need, additionally, for the strengthening and creating of organizations of Catholic doctors, lawyers, politicians, social workers, and of other professions that intersect with the public sphere of life. The creation of a third, Catholic-inspired, national political party should be strongly considered.

While definitely overlapping, these "internal" and "external" approaches are nonetheless distinct in their basic thrusts. The first is more defensive in nature, is primarily concerned with issues of successful religious socialization, and often-times is local in orientation. The latter is more offensive in nature, is primarily concerned with the formal political process, and is often national in scope. The three sociological types of Christian thought and action as presented by Ernest Troeltsch can be altered and usefully adapted in the neoconservative "mediating structures" approach to social change.[30] Troeltsch spoke of "church-like," "sect-like," and highly individualistic "mystical" religious orientations to the world. The "church-like" orientation is one geared toward the evangelization of the total culture but, in a pluralistic context, is prepared to forge common ground and compromises with philosophies not one's own. The "sect-like" orientation, precisely because it rejects the dominant ethos in the general culture and is not prepared to bargain away what it considers to be the essentials of its philosophy in a pluralistic context, withdraws to a corner of society where it can put its faith into practice in a more-or-less unadulterated manner. The "mystical" orientation, while tending in Troeltsch's analysis toward our previous discussion of "autonomous individualism," could also include a form of individualism geared to creatively but faithfully interpreting the faith but without a strong dependency on, or attachment to, any specific group or organization within the Church, with the exception of the Magisterium.

Translating Troeltsch's admittedly altered typology into our "mediating structures" analysis, one can state that all three orientations, *if effectively guided by Magisterial authority and if working cooperatively with each other,* are necessary to bring about a new Christendom through the American democratic, political process. Those organizations and individuals with a "church-like" orientation are, realistically speaking, needed in a pluralistic context like ours in which secularism holds a privileged position. Their job, basically, is to make as much of the Catholic case as is possible in both the public sphere and civil society. It is the task of those more "sect-like" Catholic organizations and groups to present fully the majesty and holiness of the Catholic religion and to make sure that the compromises and "deals" forged by the "church-like" don't violate fundamental principle and that they must be tolerated only temporarily and provisionally. And it is the task of those, relatively speaking, "socially isolated" orthodox Catholic individualists to use their God-given talents and, relatively speaking, "structurally free" positions to serve both as the honest and evenhanded critics of "church-like" and "sect-like" orientations and to suggest new modes of authentically interpreting and adapting the eternal truths of the Catholic faith to an ever changing set of historical and social circumstances.

As of the moment, one can state that the bright promise of Catholic social doctrine has failed to be implemented in American society because, in part, this three-pronged division of labor within the Catholic community is inoperative. The "Church-like" have given away the store; the "sect-like" have turned their hearts and minds too much away from what is still good or at least salvageable in American civilization and in the Catholic Church of the United States, and the orthodox individualists have been too content to act the role of dilettantes or have been allowed to hang on their solitary branches.

Notes

1. Joseph A. Varacalli, "Whose Justice and Justice for What Purpose?: A Catholic Neo-Orthodox Critique," *International Journal of Politics, Culture, and Society* 6, no. 2 (winter 1992): 309-321. Joseph A. Varacalli, "A Catholic Sociological Critique of Gustavo Gutierrez's *A Theology of Liberation*," *The Catholic Social Science Review* 1 (1996): 175-189.
2. Joseph A. Varacalli, "Catholic Conservatism–Does It Exist? Where Is It Going?" *Lay Witness* 16, no. 10 (November-December 1995): 12-13, 30.
3. Joseph A. Varacalli, "The 'Remakers' of American Catholic History," *Faith and Reason* 16, no. 4 (winter 1990): 387-403.
4. Salvatore Primeggia and Joseph A. Varacalli, "The Sacred and Profane among Italian American Catholics: The Giglio Feast," *International Journal of Politics, Culture, and Society* 9, no. 3 (spring 1996): 432-449. Joseph A. Varacalli, Salvatore Primeggia, Salvatore J. LaGumina and Donald J. D'Elia, eds., *The Saints in the Lives of Italian-Americans: An Interdisciplinary Investigation* (Stony Brook, New York: Forum Italicum, 1999). Joseph A. Varacalli, "Saints," in *The Italian-American Experience: An Encyclopedia*, Salvatore LaGumina, Frank J. Cavaioli, Salvatore Primeggia, and Joseph A. Varacalli, eds. (New York: Garland Press, 2000).
5. Primeggia and Varacalli, "The Sacred and Profane," 432-449.
6. Michael Schwartz, *The Persistent Prejudice: Anti-Catholicism in America* (Huntington, Indiana: Our Sunday Visitor, 1984).
7. Stephen M. Krason, "The New Recourse to Executive Power: Weapon of the Culture Wars," *Wanderer* (8 June 1995).
8. Rev. Richard J. Neuhaus et al., "Symposium on 'The End of Democracy?': The Judicial Usurpation of Politics,'" *First Things* 67 (November 1996): 18-42.

9. Russell Shaw, "Would the Pope Call the United States a 'Regime'?" *Our Sunday Visitor* (12 January 1997): 3.

10. Robert P. George et al., "Symposium on 'Natural Law in American Politics and Constitutional Law,'" *The Catholic Social Science Review* 1 (1996): 11-56.

11. George et al., *Natural Law*, 11-56.

12. Allan Bloom, *The Closing of the American Mind* (New York: Simon and Schuster, 1987).

13. Bryce Christensen, *Utopia against the Family: The Problems and Politics of the American Family* (San Francisco, California: Ignatius Press, 1990).

14. Joseph A. Varacalli, "Multiculturalism, Catholicism, and American Civilization," *Homiletic and Pastoral Review* 94, no. 6 (March 1994): 47-55.

15. William Rusher, *The Coming Battle for the Media* (New York: William Morrow, 1988).

16. Edward S. Herman and Noam Chomsky, *Manufacturing Consent: The Political Economy of the Mass Media* (New York: Pantheon Books, 1988).

17. S. Robert Lichter, Stanley Rothman, and Linda S. Lichter, *The Media Elite* (Chevy Chase, Maryland: Adler and Adler, 1986).

18. Rev. John Courtney Murray, *We Hold These Truths: Catholic Reflections on the American Proposition* (New York: Image Books, 1964).

19. John Rao, *Americanism and the Collapse of the Church in the United States* (St. Paul, Minnesota: Remnant Publications, 1984).

20. Joseph A. Varacalli, "Review Essay on David Blackenhorn's *Fatherless America: Confronting Our Most Urgent Social Problem,*" *Faith and Reason*, forthcoming.

21. Robert N. Bellah et al., *Habits of the Heart: Individualism and Commitment in American Life* (New York: Harper and Row, 1985).

22. David Blackenhorn, *Fatherless America: Confronting Our Most Urgent Social Problem* (New York: Basic Books, 1995), 167.

23. Rev. Richard J. Neuhaus, "The Liberalism of John Paul II," *First Things* 73 (May 1997): 18.

24. Robert P. Hunt et al., "Symposium on David Schindler v. Neoconservatism," *The Catholic Social Science Review* 3 (1998): 37-75.

25. Varacalli, "Review Essay on Blankenhorn's *Fatherless America,*" forthcoming; see also Adrian Walker's defense of David Schindler's position, "Symposium on David Schindler v. Neoconservatism," 63-68.

26. Peter L. Berger and Pastor Richard J. Neuhaus, *To Empower People: The Role of Mediating Structures in Public Policy* (Washington, D. C.: American Enterprise Institute, 1977).

27. Joseph A. Varacalli, "'Mediating Structures' and the Future of the Christian Family," in *Fighting for the Family*, Kevin Perrotta and John C. Blattner, eds. (Ann Arbor, Michigan: Center for Pastoral Renewal, 1990): 65-96. Joseph A. Varacalli, "To Empower Catholics: The Catholic League for Religious and Civil Rights as a 'Mediating Structure,'" *Nassau Review* 5, no. 4 (1988): 45-61.

28. Emile Durkheim, *The Elementary Forms of the Religious Life* (New York: Collier Books, 1965).

29. Berger and Neuhaus, *To Empower People*, 3.

30. Ernest Troeltsch, *The Social Teachings of the Christian Churches*, vol. 1 (London: George Allen and Unwin, Ltd., 1931).

Chapter Twelve

The Catholic Vision and American Populism: A Case of Elective Affinity?

Sociologist James R. Kelly asks a crucial question when he inquires as to what sectors of American society could serve, in principle, as effective carriers of the Catholic vision. As Professor Kelly points out, in and by themselves, ideas (Catholic and otherwise) are not likely to catch on and make an effective impact without the concrete support of interest groups or classes of individuals. As Professor Kelly states, "We might ask what economic class, or interest, might be the 'carrier' of the ideals of Catholic social thought, for the mere utterance of values produces no political change....We immediately realize that Catholic social thought can expect no immediate 'resonance' from any clearly defined intellectual or class interest. Catholic social thought does not easily blend into the dominant systematic Western styles of political thought."[1] The classic example of James R. Kelly's logic is offered by Max Weber through his concept of "elective affinity."[2] Martin Luther's ideas caught on in sixteenth-century Germany because they, intentionally or not, served the interests of the German princes looking to escape politically from the orbit of the Catholic world.

In contemporary America, socialist ideas have caught on in those new knowledge sectors of the American economy that claim to require an elite, gnostic-like, leadership in ideas and significant personnel to man tax supported government-sponsored or associated bureaucracies. Conversely, capitalist ideology in the United States is primarily supported by an "old business class" of prominent individuals in America's private enterprise sectors. Similarly, radical feminist ideas are influential because they support the (perceived) needs of middle to upper class professional women intent on denying nature's division of labor along gender lines. Many such sectors of American society exist that are, empirically in the short run at least, impervious to Catholic social teaching. Put crudely, evangelization efforts within the inner sanctums of the liberal Democratic Party, the Rockefeller Republican club, and the National Organization of Women are not congenial recruiting halls for the Faith. The social geography of America's culture war makes implausible, at least initially, serious inroads on certain terrains. (The major exceptions to this assertion are those secularized individuals "burned out" by the inner contradictions of their secular philosophies come home to roost and their teenaged children not yet fully socialized into either a secular ideology or careerism). In this sense, then, apostolates directed to convert secular or progressive intellectuals, like that of Rev. Richard J. Neuhaus, while important, remain necessarily secondary to those more likely to be successful, authentic, complete, and long lasting.

Who or what, then, could carry the ball for the Catholic Church in America? Most obviously, the impressive set of Church institutions (e.g., educational, social service, mass media, etc.) could serve as one effective carrier of Catholic social thought if those institutions were united and loyal to Magisterial teaching. At this juncture in time, again, they are certainly not. The first priority, then, in the goal of effective evangelization is the restoration of integrity to the Catholic house.[3]

Where, however, can the Church go when leaving the realm of her own institutions? Some real, but limited and heavily qualified, assistance might come from the non-Catholic remnants of the older and former Judaic-Christian consensus. Conservative Protestants do share, for instance, a similar social agenda with orthodox Catholics on a significant number of substantive social policy issues, although it is less likely that there is agreement on the underlying philosophy and rationale in defending such positions. Cooperative ventures and tactical alliances should be sought out with and within any number of "Christian coalitions" but Catholics should be wary of evangelistic efforts and prejudicial attitudes toward them; conversely, Catholics should not count on (while still striving for) major conversions from individuals who are themselves deeply committed to their own Christian traditions.

However, an unexplored and propitious area of evangelization for Mother Church lies within the millions of basically unchurched and nominal Christians who are part of America's working class. They are "ripe," if you will, for conversion for two reasons, one positive, one negative. Negatively, these "natural pagans" aren't corrupted by either highly articulated capitalistic or socialistic ideas; they are pragmatists who understand the selfish and elitist nature of allegiance to either of these alternatives. Positively, like *all* of God's children, they have "God's law written in their hearts." However, unlike many in the middle to upper-middle classes, the natural law is able to shine through more clearly, in both thought and action, because it is not as obstructed by systematic and antithetical ideologies opposed to the Faith. The then-Pastor Richard Neuhaus made this point brilliantly when he observed that the "natural law comes naturally to all but those who've been culturally denatured by having their minds bent to the denial of the obvious."[4] The basically good and ideologically unhindered inclinations of the working classes, however, need the Gospel of Christ and authentic Catholic doctrine to move more fully toward sanctification and Christian perfection. For one thing, and despite eschewing any abstract Enlightenment-based ideology, the working class in contemporary American society has tended to fall prey to much sexual perversity. This is so given the absence of a strong Catholic religious presence combined with the omnipresent cultural influence of Hollywood and other associated public sphere megastructural institutions (e.g., higher education, the arts) fostering the "emancipated lifestyle."

Nonetheless, the "people-oriented," "personalistic," "solidaristic" and universal thought of the Catholic Church—consistent with what Father Avery Dulles has termed the "prophetic humanism" of John Paul II[5]—would wear easily on working class sleeves (as grace builds upon and perfects nature) given the proper and sufficient exposure. It is not just that the Catholic Church has the demonstrated ability to draw out the sacred from the profane but also that she has the gift, commissioned by Christ, to uplift the ordinary to the transcendent. As Karl Adam puts it, "The Church has to raise men to God by her teaching and moral discipline."[6]

It is important to note, as an aside, that the analysis provided here rejects the Catholic neoconservative (or "right wing Americanist") position of scholars like Michael Novak, Rev. Richard John Neuhaus, and George Weigel to the effect that America's problems are coterminous with the elite secular new class. Rather, the argument here is that while the neoconservatives are correct in locating the origin of the problem, the moral decay in American culture has been widely disseminated, over the past thirty years, into the very vitals of the American middle, especially upper-middle, class. Conversely put, the infiltration process has not, as yet, fully contaminated the working to lower-middle class.

Furthermore, and even more importantly, the analysis posited here is quite consistent with the "restorationist" agenda of John Paul II. This agenda, following Paul Johnson, *rejects* the option "to retreat from the openness of the Council, retire into the fortress and lift up the drawbridge against the modern world."[7] Rather, Johnson contends:

> John Paul believes that Catholicism should assert both its doctrinal vigor and its concern for mass evangelism. The two do not exclude, they complement each other. The note he seeks to strike might be termed enlightened populism. He does not think that the great central clarities of Christianity make uncomfortable bedfellows with the pieties of the masses. Certainly they live easily in his own breast.[8]

To make reference to one of Max Weber's many useful sociohistorical concepts, there stands a natural "elective affinity" between Catholic social thought and American populism. Both bodies of thought, for one thing, stress a fundamental humanness in community whose reach is inclusive and whose nature is nontotalitarian. If this combination connects, it might very well sweep up major sections of America immediately and, eventually, the total culture. Indeed, as Catholic historian Dominic A. Aquila has argued, "a rehabilitated populism beckons us."[9] For Aquila,

> Catholics cannot comfortably participate in American politics…so long as one conceives of the political terrain solely according to the liberal and conservative axis. But there has long been a constant populist undercurrent to American politics that offers a more promising resolution to the Catholic dilemma….To be sure liberals, with some measure of truth, have heaped scorn on populist racism, provincialism, and knee-jerk patriotism but their distortions have obscured populism's more commendable features—its combination of the Left's insistence on economic justice with the Right's respect for tradition, moral responsibility, and belief in the wide ownership of productive property….The well-developed populist critique of the "expert class" also resonates well with Joseph Cardinal Ratzinger's complaint with the revisionist theologians of this class who browbeat the faithful for their grip on tradition. "The ecclesial Magisterium," says Cardinal Ratzinger, "protects the faith of the simple, of those who do not write books, who do not appear on television, and who do not write editorials in the newspapers: this is the democratic task."[10]

The best example of a recent social movement based on such an "elective affinity" was the 1992 and 1996 Republican campaign for president of Patrick J. Buchanan. The philosophical basis for his "conservatism of the heart" must further be strengthened in its rootage in Catholic social thought. Secondly, the success of his, or some other related, movement presupposes a far more orthodox leadership and united Catholic population than is presently the case.

Notes

1.   James R. Kelly, "Toward Confidence: Catholic Social Thought in North America," *Social Thought* 10, no. 2 (spring 1984): 68.

2.   Max Weber, *The Theory of Social and Economic Organization* (New York: Oxford University Press, 1947). Max Weber, *From Max Weber*, Hans C. Gerth and C. Wright Mills, eds. (New York: Oxford University Press, 1946).

3.   Joseph A. Varacalli, "Sharing or Secularizing Catholic Social Teaching?: A Reflection on the U.S.C.C. Statement, *Sharing Catholic Social Teaching: Challenges and Directions*," *Catholic Social Science Review* 4 (1999).

4.   Pastor Richard J. Neuhaus, "Recovering a Heritage and Some Common Sense," *National Catholic Register* (19 April 1987): 5.

5.   Rev. Avery Dulles, *The Prophetic Humanism of John Paul II* (New York: Fordham University Press, 1994).

6. Karl Adam, *The Spirit of Catholicism* (Garden City, New York: Image Books, 1954), 14.

7. Paul Johnson, *Pope John Paul II and the Catholic Restoration* (New York: St. Martin's Press, 1981), 191.

8. Johnson, *Pope John Paul II*, 192.

9. Dominic A. Aquila, "Review of Stephen M. Krason's *Liberalism, Conservatism, and Catholicism,*" *Social Justice Review* 83, nos. 3-4 (March/April 1992): 63.

10. Aquila, "Review of Krason," 62-63.

Chapter Thirteen

John Paul II and the Restorationists: Picking Up the Pieces for a Real Catholic Moment

America, again, has never had its "Catholic moment." And, once again at least as far as the human eye can see, the Catholic moment today is actually further away from realization than it was during the Church's heyday in post-World War II America. However, the ascendancy of Karol Wojtyla to the See of Peter in 1978 has energized the now decidedly minority orthodox camp within the Catholic Church in America to once again attempt to "restore all things—in this case, America—to Christ." The term "restorationists" has been applied to this group. The term is neither completely accurate or fair insofar as it is used to imply that the goal of the restorationists is to bring into being some form of a Catholic theocracy or the alleged good old days of a medieval Catholicism. The term is useful, however, in pointing out the restorationist goals of institutionalizing a strong Catholic/Christian presence in the public square and of co-opting and strengthening whatever is useful in modern life to promote Catholic/Christian goals (e.g., scientific or technological advance, cultural and political ideas such as democracy and the separation of Church and State properly understood, rational systems to provide mass education and health care, etc.).

Since 1978, restorationists have made steady, albeit slow and uneven, progress in implementing their vision. The many new bishops appointed during John Paul II's reign are, as a group, more orthodox and obvious in their allegiance to the historic Faith. Many among the newer cohorts of priests, sisters, and seminarians are likewise more serious, traditional, and sophisticated in their faith. Not only are the religious orders that are traditional thriving, but new orthodox orders, like the Legionaries of Christ, have recently come into existence. Opus Dei has become a major religious force on the American Catholic scene. Lay-based organizations like Catholics United for the Faith, Americans United for the Pope, the Wanderer Forum, Women for Faith and Family, and the Catholic League for Religious and Civil Rights are both growing in numbers and in their effectiveness-as evangelizers and defenders of the faith. A few new orthodox Catholic colleges have been created (Christendom, Thomas More, Thomas Aquinas, Magdalen, and soon Ave Maria) and others (Franciscan University, University of Dallas) are turning the corner back to orthodoxy. Some university departments in major Catholic institutions (Law at the University of Notre Dame, Philosophy at Catholic University of America, Christian Civilization at Gannon University) are making their presence felt, both locally and nationally. Publishing ventures like *Crisis* and *Catholic Dossier* (under Ralph McInerney's lead), *Ignatius Press* and the *Adoremus Newsletter* (under Rev. Joseph Fessio's direction), Christendom Press (led by John Jannaro), the *Homiletic and Pastoral Review* (edited by Rev. Kenneth Baker), the *Latin Mass Magazine* (originally inspired by the late William Marra and now edited by Rodger McCaffrey), and the *Wanderer* (led by Al Matt, Jr.) are flourishing and making a certain impact. Mother Angelica's EWTN television, radio, and computer highway ventures are making the Catholic Faith available across all sectors of American society. Another innovation made possible in today's sophisticated world of mass media is the creation of the International Catholic University, which offers, through the medium of electronics, the possibility of earning a college degree under the tutelage of nationally prominent orthodox Catholic scholars. Some diocesan newspapers such as *Catholic New York* and the *Sooner Catholic* of Oklahoma are not only orthodox but sophisticated. Professional organizations of intellectuals (the Fellowship of Catholic Scholars, founded 1977, under the presidency of Gerard V. Bradley), social scientists (the Society of Catholic Social Scientists, founded 1992, under the presidency of Stephen M. Krason), Catholic C.E.O.s (Legatus) founded by Thomas S. Monaghan, and other professional organizations of lawyers and medical personnel are on the rise once again. Mention should also be made of the work of Nina Shea, a Catholic who directs the Center for Religious Freedom at Freedom House in Washington, D.C. Spectacular has been the rise to prominence of the Cardinal Newman Society for the Preservation of Catholic Higher Education led by Patrick Reilly and Mo Fung. Calls for the establishment of all-purpose Catholic religious and cultural centers have been made in those areas of America where Catholic dissidents possess almost monopolistic power.[1] A few serious orthodox Catholic scholars and professionals have recently been appointed to important positions within the National Conference of Catholic Bishops/United States Catholic Conference. Simply put, some of the once impressive Catholic bureaucratic infrastructure has been retaken by forces loyal to the Faith while other "non-official" agencies have been created to promote a restorationist agenda.

However, the single most important weapon in the orthodox Catholic arsenal is John Paul II himself, both as a exemplary prophet and as author of an impressive set of encyclicals and other Catholic statements.

Speaking of John Paul II's "restorationist agenda," Paul Johnson, in 1981, observes that

> in our volatile and violent society, the existence of a great international ecclesiastical community...should be a source of comfort. That community has been sick. It is now recovering its health and energy. John Paul has been its skilled and resolute physician. But his task is not over. It may be that the more positive and original portion of it is to come. By restoring the Catholic Church to its old vigor, he is performing an important service to humanity. The presence of the genial philosopher-evangelist on St. Peter's seat in Rome is a powerful reassurance, to quote the words of Gladstone, that "the resources of civilization are not exhausted."[2]

It must be pointed out, however, that progressive Americanist forces are still in charge of much of Catholic America, although the élan, energy, and ideas are with the orthodox underdogs. As of now, the heterodox game plan is quite transparent and betrays their secular humanistic worldview: they are waiting for John Paul II to exit the scene and hope for a liberal successor much more congenial to their overall design. Orthodox Catholics, trusting in God's plan, will faithfully take what comes. Paraphrasing the famous adage of St. Ignatius of Loyola, they "will pray as if everything depends on God, but act as if everything depends on them."

Notes

1. Joseph A. Varacalli, "The Catholic Religious and Cultural Center: A Contemporary Call on Behalf of the Faith," *Fellowship of Catholic Scholars Newsletter* 18, no. 3 (July 1995): 21-26.

2. Paul Johnson, *Pope John Paul II and the Catholic Restoration* (New York: St. Martin's Press, 1981), 194-195.

Chapter Fourteen

Linking Heaven and Earth: The Catholic Contribution to Culture, Institutional Life, and the Individual

Failed community notwithstanding, Rev. Richard J. Neuhaus is correct in that the Catholic Church perennially offers mankind a bright promise; that of eternal salvation resting with the Lord in the next life and a balanced, purposeful life in this world serving God, and through God, oneself, one's family, one's local community, and one's society. Our aforementioned tripartite distinction between *culture*, *institutional life*, and the *individual* once again serves a useful, albeit imperfect, purpose in analyzing the Catholic contribution.

Culturally, the Church enriches American culture primarily two ways: first, as the standard bearer and ultimate interpreter of the natural law and, secondly, and relatedly, through her constant presentation and development of Catholic social doctrine. Regarding the first, through the natural law the Church defends the existence of purpose in nature, an objective moral order and the integrity of a holistically understood reason to lead humans to comprehend truth, exemplify holiness, appreciate beauty, and exercise discernment and prudence in the utilization of the various goods of the earth. The natural law tradition is both the primary vehicle for legitimate ecumenical relations and the primary antidote to the prevailing subjectivist therapeutic philosophies[1] reigning today, which bring in their wake so much social pathology.

Overlapping with the natural law, the social doctrine of the Church also mightily contributes to American (and world) culture. John Paul II's *Veritatis*

Splendor affirms, among many other points, that the only valid understanding of freedom involves fidelity to truth. The fundamental importance of the family as the basic unit of society is analyzed in beautiful detail in encyclicals that range from Pius XI's *Casti Connubii* (1930) to John Paul II's *Familiaris Consortio* (1981). That every conjugal act must be open to the gift of life and that the Catholic understanding of sexuality is a positive, beautiful calling between married partners is presented powerfully in Paul VI's *Humanae Vitae* (1968). Rev. Neuhaus summarizes this calling lucidly:

> The way of love is openness to the other and openness to life. It is the uncompromised gift of the other and, ultimately, to God. Against a widespread dualism that views the body as instrumental to the self, the way of love knows that the body is integral to the self. Against a sexuality in which women become objects for the satisfaction of desire, the way of love joins two persons in mutual respect and mutual duty, in which sacred bond turns to reverence and duty to delight. Against a culture in which sex is trivialized and degraded, the way of love invites eros to participate in nothing less than the drama of salvation.[2]

In Pius XI's *Divini Redemptoris* (1937), the false and pernicious nature of atheistic communism is exposed. In *Pacem in Terris* (1963), John XXIII restates the Catholic principle that the purpose of government is to promote the common good, which itself involves furthering the total person, both body and soul. *Centesimus Annus*, authored by John Paul II in 1991, provides yet another critique of both capitalist and socialist societies, defending, in a qualified manner, private property, profit, and the free market but cautioning against the consumerism and superficial gratifications found especially in the West. In *Evangelium Vitae* (1994), John Paul II calls the laity to support and further the central Catholic teachings on life. That creative, dignified work is a constitutive element in the anthropology of mankind and a prerequisite for a just social order is the key message of John Paul II's *Laborem Exercens* (1981). The fundamental rights of workers to organize and fight for a decent material and spiritual existence is laid out in the first great social encyclical, *Rerum Novarum*, authored by Pope Leo XIII in 1891. *Quadragesimo Anno* (1931), written by Pope Pius XI, follows up Leo's encyclical, elucidating the proper organizational principle of society, that is, that of subsidiarity. That the creation of an international order demands the assistance of modern societies to those more traditional in nature and that true "development" entails the recognition of more than just economic considerations is analyzed by Paul VI in his *Populorum Progressio* (1967).

Empirically speaking, there simply is not any other agency on earth that has produced such a wealth of insight on how the world does, and should, operate. What Rev. Neuhaus says of the recent encyclicals of Pope John Paul II holds true for the ever developing, ever more sophisticated, and ever more useful tradition of Catholic social doctrine, that is, it presents "the world with an ensemble of reasons to hope, of reasons to believe, of reasons to act, of reasons not to be afraid. There is nothing else even remotely like this teaching in the whole of the world."[3] These teachings, furthermore as pointed out by Stephen M. Krason,[4] are both consistent with each other and organically related. And, needless to say, the comprehensiveness and awe-inspiring scope of the social doctrine of the Church have only been lightly touched upon.

Institutionally, the Catholic Church contributes to American society by offering a series of "mediating structures"[5] that operate between, on the one hand, the individual, and on the other, the State and other public sphere megastructures (corporations, the educational and mass media establishments, etc.) whose monopolistic tendencies threaten the freedom and material and spiritual well-being of the average "alienated" modern citizen. That this institutional infrastructure must be overhauled and reenergized is an issue previously discussed. The overriding point, however, is that the Catholic community's organizational network represents, potentially, the single greatest carrier of moral authority outside of the government and corporations, and provides protection, therefore, from the totalitarian potentialities inherent in socialism and the authoritarian leanings of capitalism.

Finally, the Catholic Church does and can contribute to society through the way she (potentially) shapes *individuals*, that is, the members of her flock. The spiritual, reasonable, and balanced Catholic worldview ideally produces individuals characterized by their holiness, intellectualism, aesthetic sensibilities, and social concern. In order for the Church to more fully contribute as such, she must first be herself, faithful to her calling established and constantly reaffirmed by Jesus Christ. Therein lies the great challenge.

Notes

1. Joseph A. Varacalli, "The Failure of the Therapeutic: Implications for Society and Church," *Faith and Reason* 23, no. 1 (spring 1998): 3-22.
2. Rev. Richard J. Neuhaus, "The Catholic Moment in America," in *Catholics in the Public Square: The Role of Catholics in American Life, Culture, and Politics*, Thomas P. Melady, ed. (Huntington, Indiana: Our Sunday Visitor, 1995), 40.
3. Rev. Richard J. Neuhaus, "Can Catholic Americans Be Trusted in the Public Square?" in *Public Catholicism: The Challenge of Living the Faith in a Secular Culture*, Thomas P. Melady, ed. (Huntington, Indiana: Our Sunday Visitor, 1996), 52.
4. Stephen M. Krason, *Liberalism, Conservatism, and Catholicism: An Evaluation of Contemporary American Political Ideologies in Light of Catholic Social Teaching* (New Hope, Kentucky: Catholics United for the Faith, 1991). Stephen M. Krason, *Preserving a Good Political Order and a Democratic Republic: Reflections from Philosophy, Great Thinkers, Popes, and America's Founding Era* (New York: Mellen Press, 1998).

5.   Peter L. Berger and Pastor Richard J. Neuhaus, *To Empower People: The Role of Mediating Structures in Public Policy* (Washington, D.C.: American Enterprise Institute, 1977). Joseph A. Varacalli, "'Mediating Structures' and the Future of the Christian Family," in *Fighting for the Family*, Keving Perrotta and John C. Blattner, eds. (Ann Arbor, Michigan: Center for Pastoral Renewal, 1990), 65-96. Joseph A. Varacalli, "To Empower Catholics: The Catholic League for Religious and Civil Rights as a 'Mediating Structure,'" *Nassau Review* 5, no. 4 (1988): 45-61.

Conclusion

Staying the Course

The collapse of that truly evil empire, the Soviet Union, caught most observers by surprise even though there was, at the time, widespread recognition that Marxism as an ideology was widely repudiated by the vast majority of the relevant populations. Empirically, this gives those forces loyal to both John Paul II and the Magisterial authority he represents some real hope. A useful analogy is present: the "Americanists" may control the Church bureaucracy in the United States but it is the orthodox Catholics who possess the ideas, the energy, the will, and the faith. It *is* possible, *then*, that the hollowed out, lifeless Americanist bureaucracy *may* soon collapse as did its Soviet analogue.

However, there are no worldly guarantees. Christ has called his Catholic Americans to be faithful, not "successful" by worldly political standards. At whatever human cost the duty of faithful Catholics is to stay the course for Christ, His Church, and His human creation. In *Crossing the Threshold of Hope*, #221, John Paul II declares that Christ will give those who attempt to evangelize society the assurance of God's love: "At the end of the second millennium, we need perhaps more than ever the words of the Risen Christ: 'Be not afraid!'"[1]

Note

1.   Pope John Paul II, *Crossing the Threshold of Hope* (New York: Knopf, 1994).

Bibliography

Adam, Karl. *The Spirit of Catholicism*. Garden City, New York: Image Books, 1954.

Allport, Gordon. *The Individual and His Religion*. New York: Macmillan, 1960.

American Catholic Lawyers Association. "Do Pat Buchanan's Views Contradict Catholic Teaching?" In *The Wanderer* (21 March 1996).

Aquila, Dominic A. "Review of Stephen M. Krason's Liberalism, Conservatism, and Catholicism." *Social Justice Review* 83, nos. 3-4 (March/April 1992).

Barber, Benjamin R. "The Compromised Republic: Public Purposelessness in America." In *The Moral Foundations of the American Republic*, Robert H. Horwitz, ed. Charlottesville, Virginia: University of Virginia Press, 1977.

Bell, Daniel. *The Cultural Contradictions of Capitalism*. New York: Basic Books, 1976.

Bellah, Robert N., Richard Madsen, William M. Sullivan, Ann Swidler, and Steven M. Tipton. *Habits of the Heart: Individualism and Commitment in American Life*. Berkeley, California: University of California Press, 1985.

———. *The Good Society*. New York: Alfred A. Knopf, 1991.

Bellarmine, St. Robert. *Hell and Its Torments*. Rockford, Illinois: Tan Books, 1990.

Benestad, J. Brian. *The Pursuit of a Just Social Order: Policy Statements of the U.S. Catholic Bishops, 1966-80*. Washington, D.C.: Ethics and Public Policy Center, 1982.

Bennett, William J. *The Index of Leading Cultural Indicators*. Washington, D.C.: The Heritage Foundation, 1993.

Berger, Peter L. *The Sacred Canopy: Elements of a Sociological Theory of Religion*. New York: Doubleday and Company, 1967.

———. *Pyramids of Sacrifice: Political Ethics and Social Change*. New York: Basic Books, 1974.

———. *The Capitalist Revolution: Fifty Propositions about Prosperity, Equality, and Liberty*. New York: Basic Books, 1986.

Berger, Peter L., and Richard J. Neuhaus. *To Empower People: The Role of Mediating Structures in Public Policy*. Washington, D.C.: American Enterprise Institute, 1977.

Blankenhorn, David. *Fatherless America: Confronting Our Most Urgent Social Problem*. New York: Basic Books, 1995.

Blanshard, Paul. *American Freedom and Catholic Power*. Boston: Beacon Press, 1949.

Bloom, Alan. *The Closing of the American Mind*. New York: Simon and Schuster, 1987.

Burns, Jeffrey M. *American Catholics and the Family Crisis, 1930-1962: An Ideological and Organizational Response*. New York: Garland, 1988.

Christensen, Bryce J. *Utopia against the Family: The Problems and Politics of the American Family*. San Francisco, California: Ignatius Press, 1990.

Corbett, Julia Mitchell. *Religion in America*. Englewood Cliffs, New Jersey: Prentice Hall, 1994.

Coulson, William. "Repentant Psychologist: How I Wrecked the I.H.M. Nuns." Interview conducted by Dr. William Marra. In *The Latin Mass: Chronicles of a Catholic Reform*, special issue, 1994.

Cuddihy, John. *No Offense: Civil Religion and Protestant Taste*. New York: Seabury, 1978.

D'Elia, Donald J. *The Spirits of '76: A Catholic Inquiry*. Front Royal, Virginia: Christendom Press, 1983.

D'Elia, Donald J., and Stephen M. Krason, eds. *We Hold These Truths and More: Further Catholic Reflections on the American Proposition*. Steubenville, Ohio: Franciscan University Press, 1993.

Dolan, Jay P. *The American Catholic Experience*. New York: Doubleday, 1985.

———. "Letter to the Editor: Reply to Varacalli," *The American Historical Review* 91, no. 5 (December 1986).

Droleskey, Thomas A. "Buchanan Says He Is Only Prolife Candidate Who Can Win Nomination." In *The Wanderer* (8 February 1996).

Dulles, Avery, S.J. *Religion and the Transformation of Politics*. New York: Fordham University, 1993.

———. *The Prophetic Humanism of John Paul II*. New York: Fordham University, 1994.

Durkheim, Emile. *The Elementary Forms of the Religious Life*. New York: Collier Books, 1965.

Ellis, Monsignor John Tracy, ed. *Documents of American Catholic History*. Milwaukee: Bruce Publishing, 1956.

Finnis, John. *Natural Law and Natural Rights*. Oxford: Clarendon Press, 1980.

Fitzpatrick, James K. "Was Leo XIII a Liberal Democrat?" In *The Wanderer* (9 May 1996).

Friedman, Murray. "Religion and Politics in an Age of Pluralism, 1945-1976: An Ethnocultural View." In *Publius* 10, no. 3 (summer 1980).

Gallagher, Maggie. "Catholic Charity, but Keep It Quiet." In *New York Post* (2, June 1997).

Gallup, George Jr., and Jim Castelli. *The American Catholic People: Their Beliefs, Practices, and Values.* Garden City, New York: Doubleday, 1987.

George, Robert P. "Catholic Conscience and the Law." In *Catholics in the Public Square*, Thomas Patrick Melady, ed. Huntington, Indiana: Our Sunday Visitor, 1995.

Gerth, Hans, and C. Wright Mills, eds. *From Max Weber.* New York: Oxford University Press, 1946.

Glazer, Nathan, and Patrick J. Moynihan. *Beyond the Melting Pot: The Negroes, Puerto Ricans, Jews, Italians, and Irish of New York City.* Cambridge, Massachusetts: MIT Press, 1970.

Gleason, Philip. *Keeping the Faith: American Catholicism Past and Present.* Notre Dame, Indiana: University of Notre Dame Press, 1987.

————. *Contending with Modernity: Catholic Higher Education in the Twentieth Century.* Oxford: Oxford University Press, 1995.

Glock, Charles, and Rodney Stark. *Religion and Society in Tension.* Chicago: Rand McNally, 1965.

Greeley, Reverend Andrew M. *The Catholic Experience.* New York: Doubleday, 1967.

————. *The Communal Catholic.* New York: Seabury, 1976.

————. *The American Catholic.* New York: Basic Books, 1977.

————. *American Catholics since the Council: An Unauthorized Report.* Chicago, Illinois: The Thomas More Press, 1985.

————. *The Catholic Myth: The Behavior and Beliefs of American Catholics.* New York: Charles Scribner's Sons, 1990.

Haas, John M. "The Call of the Second Vatican Council to the Laity." In *Catholics in the Public Square,* Thomas Patrick Melady, ed. Huntington, Indiana: Our Sunday Visitor, 1995.

Hanna, Mary. *Catholics and American Politics.* Cambridge, Massachusetts: Harvard University Press, 1979.

Haynor, Anthony L., and Joseph A. Varacalli. "Sociology's Fall from Grace: The Six Deadly Sins of a Discipline at the Crossroads." In *Quarterly Journal of Ideology* 16, nos. 1-2 (June 1993).

Herberg, Will. *Protestant, Catholic, Jew: An Essay in Religious Sociology.* New York: Anchor, 1960.

Herman, Edward S., and Noam Chomsky. *Manufacturing Consent: The Political Economy of the Mass Media.* New York: Pantheon Books, 1988.

Hitchcock, James. *The Decline and Fall of Radical Catholicism.* New York: Image Books, 1972.

———. *The Pope and the Jesuits.* New York: The National Committee of Catholic Laymen, 1984.

Howard, Thomas. *Evangelical Is Not Enough: Worship of God in Liturgy and Sacrament.* 2nd ed. San Francisco, California: Ignatius Press, 1988.

Hudson, Deal W. "What Cradle Catholics Take for Granted." In *Public Catholicism: The Challenge of Living the Faith in a Secular American Culture*, Thomas P. Melady, ed. Huntington, Indiana: Our Sunday Visitor, 1996.

Hunter, James D. *Culture Wars: The Struggle to Define America.* New York: Basic Books, 1991.

———. *Before the Shooting Begins: Searching for Democracy in America's Culture War.* New York: Free Press, 1994.

John Paul II. *Crossing the Threshold of Hope.* New York: Knopf, 1994.

Johnson, Paul. *Pope John Paul II and the Catholic Restoration.* New York: St. Martin's Press, 1981.

Kelly, Monsignor George A. *The Battle for the American Church.* New York: Doubleday, 1979.

———. *The Crisis of Authority: John Paul II and the American Bishops.* Chicago, Illinois: Regnery Gateway, 1982.

———. *Inside My Father's House.* New York: Doubleday, 1989.

———. *Keeping the Church Catholic with John Paul II.* New York: Doubleday, 1990.

———. "Catholic Higher Education: Is It in or out of the Church?" In *Faith and Reason* 18, no. 1 (spring 1992).

———. *The Battle for the American Church Revisited.* San Francisco, California: Ignatius Press, 1995.

Kelly, James R. "Toward Confidence: Catholic Social Thought in North America." In *Social Thought* 10, no. 2 (spring 1984).

Kilpatrick, William Kirk. *Psychological Seduction: The Failure of Modern Psychology.* Nashville, Tennessee: Thomas Nelson Publishers, 1983.

Kirk, Russell. *The Roots of the American Order.* LaSalle, Illinois: Open Court Publishing, 1974.

Krason, Stephen M. *Liberalism, Conservatism, and Catholicism: An Evaluation of Contemporary American Political Ideologies in Light of Catholic Social Teaching.* New Hope, Kentucky: Catholics United for the Faith, 1991.

———. "The New Recourse to Executive Power: Weapon of the Culture Wars." In *The Wanderer* (8 June 1995).

————. *Preserving a Good Political Order and Democratic Republic: Reflections from Philosophy, Great Thinkers, Popes, and America's Founding Era.* New York: Mellen Press, 1998.

Krason, Stephen M., and Joseph A. Varacalli, "The Society of Catholic Social Scientists: Calling and Invitation." In *Social Justice Review* 84, nos. 1-2 (January-February 1993).

Lichter, S. Robert, Stanley Rothman, and Linda S. Lichter. *The Media Elite.* Chevy Chase, Maryland: Adler and Adler, 1986.

Likoudis, Paul. "Experts Agree: It's Time for Bishops to Pull Their Heads from the Sand." In *The Wanderer* (27 March 1997).

MacIntyre, Alasdair. *After Virtue: A Study in Moral Theory.* Notre Dame, Indiana: University of Notre Dame Press, 1984.

McCann, Dennis P. *New Experiment in Democracy: The Challenge for American Catholicism.* Kansas City, Missouri: Sheed and Ward, 1987.

McInerny, Ralph. *A First Glance at St. Thomas Aquinas: A Handbook for Peeping Thomists.* Notre Dame, Indiana: University of Notre Dame Press, 1990.

Melady, Thomas P. "From a Lonely Minority to a Strong Presence." In *Public Catholicism: The Challenge of Living the Faith in a Secular Culture,* Thomas P. Melady, ed. Huntington, Indiana: Our Sunday Visitor, 1996.

Morrissey, Gerard. *The Crisis of Dissent.* Front Royal, Virginia: Christendom Publications, 1985.

Murray, John Courtney, S.J. *We Hold These Truths: Catholic Reflections on the American Proposition.* New York: Image Books, 1964.

Myers, Kenneth A., ed. *Aspiring to Freedom: Commentaries on John Paul II's Encyclical "The Social Concerns of the Church"* Grand Rapids, Michigan: Eerdmans, 1988.

Neuhaus, Pastor Richard J. *The Catholic Moment: The Paradox of the Church in the Postmodern World.* San Francisco, California: Harper and Row, 1987.

————. "Recovering a Heritage and Some Common Sense." In *National Catholic Register* (19 April 1987).

Neuhaus, Reverend Richard J. "The Catholic Moment in America." In *Catholics in the Public Square: The Role of Catholics in American Life, Culture, and Politics,* Thomas P. Melady, ed. Huntington, Indiana: Our Sunday Visitor, 1995.

————. "Can Catholic Americans Be Trusted in the Public Square?" In *Public Catholicism: The Challenge of Living The Faith in a Secular Culture,* Thomas P. Melady, ed. Huntington, Indiana: Our Sunday Visitor, 1996.

————. "The Liberalism of John Paul II." In *First Things,* no. 73 (May 1997).

Niebuhr, H. R. *Christ and Culture.* New York: Harper and Row, 1951.

Novak, Michael. *The Spirit of Democratic Capitalism.* New York: Simon and Schuster, 1982.

———. "The Rediscovery of Our American Catholic Heritage." In *Catholics in the Public Square,* Thomas Patrick Melady, ed. Huntington, Indiana: Our Sunday Visitor, 1995.

O'Kane, James. "A Sociological View of U.S. Catholicism." In *Teaching the Catholic Faith: Central Questions for the 90s,* Monsignor Eugene V. Clark, ed. New York: St. John's University Press, 1991.

Peterson, David J. "Should America Examine the Morality of Free Trade?" In *The Wanderer* (8 February 1996).

Popenoe, David. "The American Family Crisis." In *Taking Sides: Clashing Views on Controversial Social Issues.* 9th ed., Kurt Finsterbusch and George McKenna, eds. Guilford, Connecticut: Dushkin, 1996.

Primeggia, Salvatore, and Joseph A. Varacalli. "The Sacred and Profane among Italian American Catholics: The Giglio Feast." In *International Journal of Politics, Culture, and Society* 9, no. 3 (spring 1996).

Rao, John. *Americanism and the Collapse of the Church in the United States.* St. Paul, Minnesota: Remnant Publications, 1984.

Reed, Ralph, Jr. "Catholic/Evangelical Relations." In *Public Catholicism: The Challenge of Living the Faith in a Secular Culture,* Thomas P. Melady, ed. Huntington, Indiana: Our Sunday Visitor, 1996.

Reichley, A. James. *Religion in American Public Life.* Washington, D.C.: The Brookings Institution, 1985.

Rice, Charles E. "Why Pat Should Go." In *The Wanderer* (25 April 1996).

Riesman, David, Nathan Glazer, and Reuel Denny. *The Lonely Crowd: A Study of the Changing American Character.* New Haven, Connecticut: Yale University Press, 1961.

Rueda, Rev. Enrique T., and Michael Schwartz. *Gays, AIDS, and You.* Old Greenwich, Connecticut: The Devin Adair Company, 1987.

Rusher, William. *The Coming Battle for the Media.* New York: William Morrow, 1988.

Salvaterra, David L. *American Catholicism and the Intellectual Life.* New York: Garland, 1988.

Schram, Glenn N. "Toward a New American Civil Theology." In *The Wanderer* (6 June 1996).

Schwartz, Michael. *The Persistent Prejudice: Anti-Catholicism in America.* Huntington, Indiana: Our Sunday Visitor, 1984.

Shaw, Russell. "Would the Pope Call the United States a 'Regime'?" In *Our Sunday Visitor* (12 January 1997).

Shils, Edward A. "Primordial, Personal, Sacred, and Civil Ties." In *Center and Periphery: Essays in Macro Sociology.* Chicago, Illinois: University of Chicago Press, 1975.

Sigmund, Paul E. *Natural Law in Political Thought.* Lanham, Maryland: University Press of America, 1971.

Smith, Monsignor William B. "Questions Answered: Cooperation Revisited." In *Homiletic and Pastoral Review* 97, no. 4 (January 1970).

————. "Questions Answered: Cooperation in Health Care." In *Homiletic and Pastoral Review* 96, no. 10 (July 1996).

Sorokin, Pitirim A. *Altruistic Love: A Study of American "Good Neighbors" and Christian Saints*. Boston, Massachusetts: Beacon, 1950.

Symposium on David Schindler v. Neoconservatism. (Contributors: Robert P. Hunt, Mark Lowery, Adrian Walker, and Kenneth L. Grasso). In *The Catholic Social Science Review* 3 (1998).

Symposium on Natural Law in American Politics and Constitutional Law. (Contributors: Robert P. George, William Bentley Ball, Stephen M. Krason, Rev. Francis Canavan, S.J., Gerard V. Bradley, David Forte, and Russell Kirk.) In *The Catholic Social Science Review* 1 (1996).

Symposium on the End of Democracy?: The Judicial Usurpation of Politics. (Contributors: Rev. Richard J. Neuhaus, Robert H. Bork, Russell Hittinger, Hadley Arkes, Charles Colson, and Robert George.) In *First Things*, no. 67 (November 1996).

Thomas, W. I., and Dorothy S. Thomas. *The Child in America: Behavior Problems*. New York: Knopf, 1928.

Troeltsch, Ernest. *The Social Teaching of the Christian Churches*. Vol. 1. Olive Wyon, trans. London: George Allen and Unwin Ltd., 1931.

Varacalli, Joseph A. *Toward the Establishment of Liberal Catholicism in America*. Lanham, Maryland: University Press of America, 1983.

————. "Book Review of Jay P. Dolan's *The American Catholic Experience*." In *The American Historical Review* 91, no. 3 (June 1986).

————. "Reply to Jay P. Dolan." In *The American Historical Review* 91, no. 5 (December 1986).

————. "The State of the American Catholic Laity: Propositions and Proposals." In *Faith and Reason* 13, no. 2 (summer 1987).

————. "Review of Dennis P. McCann's *New Experiment in Democracy*." In *Homiletic and Pastoral Review* 88, no. 10 (July 1988).

————. "A Catholic Plausibility Structure." In *Homiletic and Pastoral Review* 89, no. 2 (November 1988).

————. "To Empower Catholics: The Catholic League for Religious and Civil Rights as a 'Mediating Structure.'" In *Nassau Review* 5, no. 4 (1988).

————. "The Constitutive Elements of the Idea of an 'American' Catholic Church." In *Social Justice Review* 80, nos. 5-6 (May-June 1989).

————. "Review Essay on Judith Wallerstein and Sandra Blakeslee's *Second Chances: Men, Women, and Children a Decade after Divorce*." In *Fellowship of Catholic Scholars Newsletter* 13, no. 1 (December 1989).

————. "'Those Were the Days': Church and American Society in the 1940s and 1950s." In *Faith and Reason* 16, no. 1 (spring 1990).

————. "'Mediating Structures' and the Future of the Christian Family." In *Fighting for the Family*, Kevin Perrotta and John C. Blattner, eds. Ann Arbor, Michigan: Center for Pastoral Renewal, 1990.

————. "Review: The 'Remakers' of American Catholic History." In *Faith and Reason* 16, no. 4 (winter 1990).

————. "Renewing the Battle to Restore Sociology and the Social Sciences in Christ." In *Fellowship of Catholic Scholars Newsletter* 14, no. 3 (June 1991).

————. "Sociology, Catholicism, and Andrew Greeley." In *Law Witness* 13, no. 9 (June 1992).

————. "Whose Justice and Justice for What Purpose?: A Catholic Neo-Orthodox Critique." In *International Journal of Politics, Culture, and Society* 6, no. 2 (winter 1992).

————. "Secular Sociology's War against *Familiaris Consortio* and the Traditional Family: Whither Catholic Higher Education and Catholic Sociology?" In *The Church and the Universal Catechism*, Rev. Anthony J. Mastroeni, ed. Steubenville, Ohio: Franciscan University Press, 1992.

————. "Review of Patrick H. McNamara's *Conscience First, Tradition Second: A Study of Young American Catholics.*" In *Sociological Analysis* 53, no. 4 (winter 1992).

————. "Multiculturalism, Catholicism, and American Civilization." In *Homiletic and Pastoral Review* 94, no. 6 (March 1994).

————. "'Homophobia' at Seton Hall University: Sociology in Defense of the Faith." In *Faith and Reason* 20, no. 3 (fall 1994).

————. "The Catholic Religious and Cultural Center: A Contemporary Call on Behalf of the Faith." In *Fellowship of Catholic Scholars Newsletter* 18, no. 3 (July 1995).

————. "Divided We Fall—Unwelcome Conclusions: Review Essay on Peter Brimelow's *Alien Nation: Common Sense about America's Immigration Disaster.*" In *Crisis* 13 (November 1995).

————. "Catholic Conservatism—Does It Exist? Where Is It Going?" In *Lay Witness* 16, no. 10 (November/December 1995).

————. *The Catholic and Politics in Post-World War II America: A Sociological Analysis.* St. Louis, Missouri: Society of Catholic Social Scientists, 1995.

————. "The Contemporary Culture War in America: Whither Natural Law, Catholic Style?" In *Faith and Reason* 21, no. 4 (winter 1995).

————. "A Catholic Sociological Critique of Gustavo Gutierrez's *A Theology of Liberation.*" In *The Catholic Social Science Review* 1 (1996).

————. "The Society of Catholic Social Scientists: Catholic Social Science and the Reconstruction of the Social Order." In *Faith and Reason* 22, nos. 1-2 (spring-summer 1996).

————. "The Failure of the Therapeutic: Implications for Society and Church." In *Faith and Reason* 23, no. 1 (spring 1997).

————. "Catholic Social Science, Language, and William Brennan: Initial Reflections and Key Questions." In *Language and Faith*, Rev. Anthony J. Mastroeni, ed. Steubenville, Ohio: Franciscan University Press, 1997.

————. "Obstructing *Ex corde Ecclesiae*." In *Faith and Reason* 23, no. 3-4 (1997-1998).

————. "The Saints in the Lives of Italian-American Catholics: Toward a Realistic Multiculturalism." In *The Saints in the Lives of Italian-Americans: An Interdisciplinary Investigation*, Joseph A. Varacalli, Salvatore Primeggia, Salvatore J. LaGumina, and Donald J. D'Elia, eds. Stony Brook, New York: Forum Italicum, 1999.

————. "Saints." In *The Italian-American Experience: An Encyclopedia*, Salvatore J. LaGumina, Frank J. Cavaioli, Salvatore Primeggia, and Joseph A. Varacalli, eds. New York: Garland Press, 2000.

————. "Sharing or Secularizing Catholic Social Thinking?: A Reflection on the U.S.C.C. Statement, *Sharing Catholic Social Teaching: Challenges and Directions*." In *The Catholic Social Science Review* 4 (1999).

————. "Review Essay on David Blankenhorn's *Fatherless America: Confronting Our Most Urgent Social Problem*." In *Faith and Reason*, forthcoming.

Vitz, Paul C. "An American Disaster: Moral Relativity." In *In Search of a National Morality*, William Bentley Ball, ed. Grand Rapids, Michigan: Baker House, 1992.

Warner, Michael. *Changing Witness: Catholic Bishops and Public Policy, 1917-1994*. Washington, D.C.: Ethics and Public Policy Center, 1995.

Weber, Max. *The Theory of Social and Economic Organization*. New York: Oxford University Press, 1947.

Weigel, George. *Tranquillitas Ordinis: The Present Failure and Future Promise of American Catholic Thought on War and Peace*. Oxford: Oxford University Press, 1987.

Wilcox, Clyde, and Leopoldo Gomez. "The Christian Right and the Prolife Movement: An Analysis of the Sources of Political Support." In *Review of Religious Research* 31, no. 4 (June 1990).

Wrenn, Monsignor Michael J. *Catechisms and Controversies: Religious Education in the Postconciliar Years*. San Francisco: Ignatius Press, 1991.

Index

Adam, Karl, 44, 51-53, 101
Adoremus Newsletter, 106
Albertus Magnus Guild, 19
American Catholic Church defined, 81
American Catholic Historical
 Association, 19
American Catholic Lawyers
 Association, 16
American Catholic Philosophical
 Association, 19
American Catholic Psychological
 Association, 19
American Catholic Sociological
 Association, 19
American Constitution, 89
American Dream, 62
American populism, 99
American public order, ix, xii
American public square, 74
American working class, 100
Americanism, Americanizer,
 Americanist, x, 41, 57, 65, 77, 80-
 81, 85, 87, 113; as example of
 modernism and assimilation, 62
Americans United for the Pope, 95, 106
apostolic succession, 66
Aquila, Dominic, 102
Aristotelian tradition, 34
Arkes, Hadley, 88

autonomous self, x
Ave Maria College, 106

Baker, Rev. Kenneth, 106
Ball, William Bentley, 89
Baltimore Councils and Plenary
 Sessions, 56
Barber, Benjamin, 32
Battle for the American Church, xiv, 39
*Battle for the American Church
 Revisited*, xiv
Batule, Rev. Robert, xiii
Bell, Daniel, 31-32; cultural drive of
 modernity, 32; capitalist economic
 impulse, 32
Bellah, Robert N. xiv, 28, 31, 32, 91
Benestad, J. Brian, 67
Bennett, William J., 29
Berger, Peter L.: dissertation, xiii;
 Pyramids of Sacrifice, 15; sacred
 canopy, 32; plausibility structure
 defined, 55; secularization, 65;
 private sphere institutions and
 mediating structures, 93-94
Bernardin, Joseph Cardinal, 81
Bible, 48
Bishops' Program for Social
 Reconstruction, 62
Blankenhorn, David, 91

125

About the Author

Dr. Joseph A. Varacalli, presently Professor of Sociology at Nassau Community College—S.U.N.Y., is the executive secretary of the Society of Catholic Social Scientists. He served formerly as editor-in-chief of the *Catholic Social Science Review*, board of directors member of the Fellowship of Catholic Scholars, assistant director of the Nassau Community College Center for Italian-American Studies, and executive council member and national membership chairman of the American Italian Historical Association. In 1992, Dr. Varacalli cofounded (along with Stephen M. Krason of Franciscan University) the Society of Catholic Social Scientists.

Dr. Varacalli has authored or coauthored over 250 individual scholarly pieces in a wide variety of journals and magazines. He is the author of *Toward the Establishment of Liberal Catholicism in America* (1983) and *The Catholic and Politics in Post-World War II America: A Sociological Analysis* (1995). He is the coeditor of *The Saints in the Lives of Italian-Americans: An Interdisciplinary Investigation* (1999) and *The Italian-American Experience: An Encyclopedia* (2000).

He and his wife, Lillian, have three children: Thomas F. X. (age 10), John Paul (age 8), and Theresa Elizabeth (age 6). The Varacalli family resides on Long Island, New York.